FRANCO BERTONI

MINIMALIST ARCHITECTURE

BIRKHÄUSER – PUBLISHERS FOR ARCHITECTURE
BASEL · BOSTON · BERLIN

DoGi

PRODUCED BY
DOGI SPA, ITALIA

ORIGINAL TITLE
ARCHITETTURA MINIMALISTA

EDITOR
FRANCO CANTINI

TEXT
FRANCO BERTONI

COPY-EDITING
FRANCESCO MILO

GRAPHIC DESIGN
SEBASTIANO RANCHETTI

ORIGINAL ITALIAN EDITION: © 2002 DOGI SPA - FIRENZE - ITALY

THE LIBRARY
THE SURREY INSTITUTE OF ART & DESIGN

TRANSLATION:
FROM ITALIAN INTO ENGLISH: LUCINDA BYATT, EDINBURGH
FROM SPANISH INTO ENGLISH (TEXT ALBERTO CAMPO BAEZA): PAUL HAMMOND, BARCELONA

A CIP CATALOGUE RECORD FOR THIS BOOK IS AVAILABLE FROM THE LIBRARY OF CONGRESS, WASHINGTON D.C., USA.

DEUTSCHE BIBLIOTHEK CATALOGING-IN-PUBLICATION DATA

MINIMALIST ARCHITECTURE / FRANCO BERTONI [TRANSL.: LUCINDA BYATT - PAUL HAMMOND]. - BASEL ; BOSTON ; BERLIN : BIRKHÄUSER, 2002
DT. AUSG. U.D.T.: MINIMALISTISCHE ARCHITEKTUR
ISBN 3-7643-6642-7

THIS WORK IS SUBJECT TO COPYRIGHT. ALL RIGHTS ARE RESERVED, WHETHER THE WHOLE OR PART OF THE MATERIAL IS CONCERNED, SPECIFICALLY THE RIGHTS OF TRANSLATION, REPRINTING, RE-USE OF ILLUSTRATIONS, RECITATION, BROADCASTING, REPRODUCTION ON MICROFILMS OR IN OTHER WAYS, AND STORAGE IN DATA BASES.
FOR ANY KIND OF USE PERMISSION OF THE COPYRIGHT OWNER MUST BE OBTAINED.

© 2002 BIRKHÄUSER - PUBLISHERS FOR ARCHITECTURE, P.O. BOX 133, CH-4010 BASEL, SWITZERLAND.
MEMBER OF THE BERTELSMANNSPRINGER PUBLISHING GROUP.
THIS BOOK IS ALSO AVAILABLE IN A GERMAN LANGUAGE EDITION (ISBN 3-7643-6651-6).
PRINTED ON ACID-FREE PAPER PRODUCED FROM CHLORINE-FREE PULP. TCF ∞
PRINTED IN ITALY
ISBN 3-7643-6642-7

724.7BER

9 8 7 6 5 4 3 2 1   WWW.BIRKHAUSER.CH

CONTENTS

Minimalist Architecture

Minimalisms

The term Minimalism was coined, above all, as a means of describing in laudatory terms or in a reductive and strongly critical manner the works by protagonists of the American art scene in the late Fifties and Sixties, like Donald Judd, Sol Le Witt, Robert Morris, Richard Serra, Dan Flavin. These figures in fact used formal austerity and a marked reduction in expressive media to counter the exuberance of Abstract Expressionism or Action Painting and the aesthetic compromises brought about by the phenomena of mass culture typical of Pop Art. The same term was then used to describe phenomena in a wide variety of fields: from music to theatre, literature, architecture, graphics, design and even fashion, not to mention dance, cinema and photography. Moreover, these expressive spheres rarely came into contact and were characterised by very different features, but they were grouped together for a very brief period, one that acquired remarkable importance owing to the strong acceleration that characterised and distinguished the varied and contradictory panorama of international art at the end of last century.

Exceptions include the theatrical collaboration between Robert Wilson and Philip Glass for *Einstein on the Beach* in 1976 and *the CIVIL warS* of 1983 or, in the field of fashion, the attention focused by Giorgio Armani, the master of essential linearism, both on Robert Wilson, to whom he entrusted the choreography of his major shows (*G.A. Story* to mark the Fiftieth Anniversary of Pitti Uomo in Florence in 1976 and the recent installation at the Guggenheim in New York), and on Claudio Silvestrin who designed his most prestigious show-rooms (Paris 1999, Milan 2000, San Paolo 2001).

Additional confirmation of the pivotal role played by the world of fashion at particular moments is shown by Calvin Klein's interest in Claudio Silvestrin and John Pawson, in particular, or Issey Miyake's in Shiro Kuramata.

While in the artistic field Minimalism can, broadly speaking, be dated back to the early Sixties, with virtually no interruptions and, on the contrary, the New Minimalism of the early Nineties attracted renewed attention from the public and critics, the first convincing theatrical demonstrations by Robert Wilson did not appear until the early Seventies.[1] Leaving aside in this instance the contribution made by John Cage, the first appearances on the musical scene by La Monte Young and Terry Riley (respectively in the late Fifties and early Sixties) or by Steve Reich and Philip Glass (mid and late Sixties) varied

1. John Pawson, Van Royen apartment, London, 1986 • 2. Claudio Silvestrin, Barker-Mill apartment, London, 1993

considerably in chronological terms, whereas the term musical Minimalism was only coined in 1968 by Michael Nyman, writing as a critic, and his first works as a composer were not performed until 1976.[2]

In the literary field, the minimalist phenomenon found substantial and meaningful expression in the early works by Raymond Carver, published under the title *Will You Please be Quiet, Please?* in 1976. Carver was regarded as the leading figure of literary Minimalism, even if the sudden and explosive success of authors like Bret Easton Ellis, David Leavitt, Amy Hempel, Jay McInerney significantly slowed the pace of his achievement.

Lastly, the emergence of minimalist design was transversal, interstitial and, as in the field of architecture, transnational: it ranged from Donald Judd's first works in the furniture sector in 1978, which were later perfected in 1994, to the design consistency of AG Fronzoni dating back to 1964 if not earlier; from the famous chairs and theatrical props designed by Robert Wilson to the industrial designs by Claudio Silvestrin and John Pawson in the late Nineties.[3]

In architecture the phenomenon was recognised and labelled above all in the mid Eighties (*London Minimum* by H. Ypma, 1996), before being used to describe the earliest projects by architects like John Pawson and Claudio Silvestrin, and to reclassify the works by Tadao Ando at least ten years earlier. In this sort of anomalous movement of continuous formation and reconsideration, it even included the exciting results of Luis Barragan's later works dating from the mid Fifties and mid Sixties, which were first recognised and drawn to international attention in the exhibition organised by Emilio Ambasz at the Museum of Modern Art in New York in 1976.

These few concise examples outline a phenomenon in progress rather than a movement defined by precise dates, programmes, manifestos, and clear and explicit programmatic intentions. Its progress in bursts over time, separated by real or apparent pauses, or being conveyed from one discipline to another, not to mention the shift away from its privileged American origins and establishment in Europe and the East, are all symptomatic of the gradual formation of a sort of minimalist identity, or "minimal simplicity",[4] characterised by endless permutations and a wide variety of motivations.

If we add that virtually none of the protagonists in the various fields described above intends to conclude his output within this term, we are bound to question the legitimacy of its use as an adjective.

The minimalist label has even been rejected by the American artists themselves, who

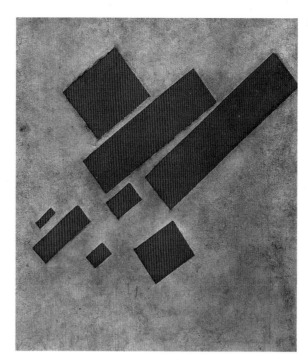

3. Josef Hoffmann, Decorative frieze for the 14th exhibition of the Secession, Vienna, 1902 • 4. Kasimir Malevic, Eight red rectangles, 1915 • 5. Carl Andre, 8 cuts, 1967 • 6. Carl Andre, Installation, 1967

in fact did not elaborate any programmes or manifestos, but were subject to a word that was first used as an artistic term in 1937 by the artist John Graham: "Minimalism is the reducing of painting to the minimum ingredients for the sake of discovering the ultimate, logical destination of painting in the process of abstracting",[5] and given legitimate standing, with greater respectability, by Richard Wollheim in his essay on *Minimal Art* in 1966. For Carl Andre (1959): "Art excludes what is not necessary"; to which he added, twenty years later: "This is the only meaning that 'minimalism' has for me".

However, the term permeated critical jargon where it was frequently used to "recall, collect and classify particular works from the recent past",[6] substituting more specific but certainly less effective labels, like ABC Art, Primary Structures or Specific Objects. It became firmly fixed in collective memory and has spread further in everyday language than its own original premise and intentions.

To quote Raymond Carver: "This whole story of minimalism has gone completely beyond the limit. We should stop using labels. A writer must be judged by what he produces and that's all".[7] However, at the same time he also confesses: "It's difficult to be simple. Every story I write goes through up to fifteen drafts".[8] Drafts that, as Carver himself underlines, entail a gradual process of narrative and verbal paring down in an

attempt to reach not only the bones, but the very marrow of the story. This is based on elimination, a process in which his editor Gordon Lish initially played a significant part, helping to draw international attention to his terse and highly effective prose.

"And what about Minimalism? Minimalism existed in other arts, it was in the air... The artists in the Sixties started reducing figuration to elementary lines, what the Americans call basic, in a space empty of significance: sculptors reduced sculpture to a geometric and metaphysical structure, and painters reduced painting to a mathematical and metaphysical structure.

In the same climate, but with colossal differences Carver reduced events to metaphysical states, basic signs, and he set them in a social vacuum... His stories could happen anywhere, but however they are almost always set inside a house, around a kitchen table or in front of a television: they are stories that take place in scenes condensed on a vivisection table, where emotion is generated by the suspense of an event that occurs in a total vacuum, for whose logic we are unprepared, rather (but very vaguely) like some of Edward Hopper's pictures".[9]

Carver's characters carry out their actions in a sort of physical and social vacuum, in which all modes of perception and behaviour are completed and revealed in such an

unusual manner that they unexpectedly reveal their most profound, almost original aspects. Carver himself gives the best definition of the aim of his own work: "If we're lucky, writer and reader alike, we'll finish the last line or two of a short story and then just sit for minute, quietly. Ideally, we'll ponder what we've just written or read; maybe our heart or our intellects will have been moved off the peg just a little from where they were before. Our body temperature will have gone up, or down, by a degree. Then, breathing evenly and steadily once more, we'll collect ourselves, writers and readers alike, get up, 'created of warm blood and nerves', as a Chekhov character puts it, and go on to the next thing: Life. Always life".[10]

Moving beyond appearances, Carver's work, like Chekhov's, is dominated by a love for life, not overburdened by Hemingway's vital exuberance or the strong tones of London epopee, but rather rooted in the humble and miserable recesses of common, and sometimes poor, squalid and difficult everyday life, and he plays to it with using the simplest instruments, which are also the most effective.

In the short story *The Errand*, published in 1986 in the collection entitled *Elephant and other stories*, Carver describes the last few hours in the life of his favourite author, Chekhov; he tells how, in an apparently banal gesture, the young maid had picked up the cork from the champagne bottle with which the Russian writer had given his farewell salute to life a few moments before dying. A simple gesture carried out by a minor character in the story, but one that sums up the handing down of an artistic inheritance and a sense of attachment to life even, and above all, when faced with its most tragic moments.

By eliminating all connotative references from his stories, Carver suspends the terse dialogues and few actions of his characters in a social and environmental vacuum, thus distilling the eternal and basic questions about the meaning of life.

The criticism of the pompous patriarch Leo Tolstoy: "Where do your characters lead you?", once made to Chekhov, "From the sofa to the storeroom and back again", is not seen as diminutive by Carver but, on the contrary, it gives substance, through the "giant from Jasnaya Polyana's" disparaging answer to his own question, to the human depth of Chekhov's literary works. As if the most important moments in everyone's life were not spent in bed, in a room, in interior silence and without great actions or great certainties.

In his *Essay on Chekhov*, Thomas Mann does not fail to remark on Anton Chekhov's deep-felt love of life, expressed through his practical and social commitment as a doc-

7. Carl Andre, Equivalent I—VIII, 1966 • 8. Donald Judd, Untitled, 1972 • 9. Robert Morris, Installation, 1964 • 10. Claudio Silvestrin, Barker-Mill apartment, London, 1993

tor and, at the same time, through his constant and uneasy literary questioning "What shall I do?", the only possible answer to which was an "Upon my honour and conscience, I don't know".

It is precisely this very human admission of impotence, this serene and melancholy acceptance of the simple facts of existence, which constitutes one of the reasons for Chekhov's contemporary success.

Thomas Mann ends the affectionate lines dedicated to the Russian author with a sort of spiritual testament: "Nevertheless, one goes on working, telling stories, giving form to truth, hoping darkly, sometimes almost confidently, that truth and serene form will avail to set free the human spirit and prepare mankind for a better, lovelier, worthier life".[11] There is an extraordinary consonance between the words of Thomas Mann and an excerpt from one of the rare writings by AG Fronzoni (the only radically minimalist Italian designer, according to Vanni Pasca): "Form is beauty, someone said that beauty will save man; I don't know if this is true, but I know that I find form very useful, indispensable and even precious, to send a message which is a thought message".[12] Truth and the serene form invoked by Thomas Mann and AG Fronzoni's thought message ("loyal, correct, essential, one that conveys what is important") [13] can only lead to

a sort of ethics of simplicity. A simplicity that exalts the true values of life and eliminates all that is superfluous and misleading around us and obscures recognition of the essential.

In architecture, Minimalism pursues this essential quality as a prime objective. Adolf Loos, in an attack against the "bad taste of modern artists" and houses decorated by architects from the schools of applied arts, had already singled it out as essential: "When I enter a house of this kind, I always pity the individuals who spend their lives there. Is this the scenario that people would have chosen for the small joys and great tragedies of their existence?!! Would it have been like this? These houses fit you like a rented Pierrot fancy-dress costume! I hope that serious events of life will never touch you, opening your eyes to your borrowed rags! (…) Just try to imagine what birth and death must be like in one of Olbrich's bedrooms, how the cry of pain of a wounded son would sound, the agonising death-rattle of a dying mother, the last thoughts of a daughter who has decided to die. (…) A letter on the table. A letter of farewell. Is the room in which this scene takes place one of good taste? Who will worry? It's a room and that's all!

But what if the room is furnished by Van de Velde?

In that case, it is not a room.
In that case, it's ….
Well, what is it then?
An insult to death!
May you always enjoy the small pleasures of life!" [14]

And what of architecture? By repressing everything around us that is not authentic, the architecture of simplicity, minimalist architecture, attempts to draw us back to a different way of living and feeling, one that is calmer, more serene, more worthy.

The apparent apartheid that connotes the work of masters like Adolf Loos or Luis Barragan, at the very end of the last century eludes the great ideological, political and formal themes used to classify the meaning of the discipline and insistently reproposes the need for a pause, a degree of detachment, that necessary distance which allows the next action to be reconsidered.

Minimalist architecture is characterised by a formal vacuum and expressive silence.
A few, eternal and fundamental questions dominate the new formal vocabulary.
The architectural silence of Adolf Loos, Louis Kahn, Luis Barragan, AG Fronzoni, Claudio Silvestrin, John Pawson, Peter Zumthor, Alberto Campo Baeza, Eduardo Souto de Moura, Tadao Ando and Michael Gabellini can be interpreted both as an intentional and motivated abstention from contingencies, or as an opening to dialogue with more extensive spiritual dimensions. The latter has for many years been absent from the panorama of a discipline that is increasingly bound by claims of social representativeness or a constantly disenchanted sociopolitical commitment. The atemporality of a few eternal questions dominates a programme that calls for mental and physical void as the necessary condition for the manifestation of a new way of living.

Showing considerable anticipation, Louis Kahn started to experiment with the void, as suggested to him by Luis Barragan, in the courtyard of the Salk Laboratories at La Jolla, California in 1959–63 and, in the same work, he also inserted a few empty volumes, a prelude to the more radical *Concrete works* installed by Donald Judd outside the Chinati Foundation in Marfa, Texas in 1992. While these facts do not undermine the record held by artistic Minimalism in the development of a severe criticism of aesthetic superfluity, they at least serve to backdate the need for formal purity and a physical vacuum in which to try out new and innovative forms of perception. Not the rapid and distracted perception of what is transient and inauthentic, but the simple and immediate perception of basic, physical and spiritual values, like time, space and silence.

11. Louis Kahn, Salk Institute for Biological Studies, La Jolla, California, 1959–65 • 12. Donald Judd, Concrete works, Chinati Foundation, Marfa, Texas, 1992 • 13. Donald Judd, Installation, Chinati

The dissatisfaction and unease generated in all social groups by contemporary consumer society, which sees the possession of material goods and their exaltation, totally unrelated to their necessity or usefulness, as the only support for a perverse logic of self-maintenance and inward growth, can be taken as the social and historical basis for the claims made by minimalist art and, in particular, for those architectural experiences that based the purpose of their existence on reduction, simplicity and a search for the essence.

Having initially been a reaction to the nightmare of the supermarket and excess, in its architectural form Minimalism is now finding goals that go further than the pure, simple motive of denunciation and instead move towards concrete attempts, albeit thinly scattered over time and space and in modest quantities, to introduce a life more imbued with spirituality, clarity and harmony.

Technology and man

Letters from Lake Como was the title given by Romano Guardini, a priest who had held the Chair of Christian Philosophy and Catholic Weltanschauung at Berlin University since 1923 and who played such an important role in Mies van der Rohes ideological and spiritual formation,[15] to a series of reflections, dating from 1926, on the destiny of a society now dominated by technology. A technology that sets no targets because "its progress takes the form of gaining ground through its own results, with no prospect of reaching any goal other than its own expansion".[16]

The growing unease that arose following the disappearance of the unity which had governed culture and forms in the period immediately prior to this invasion of the machine is clearly summarised in one of the first chapters in the book: "As I walked through the valleys of Brianza… I could not believe my eyes. Everywhere it was an inhabited land, valleys and slopes dotted with hamlets and small towns. All nature had been given a new shape by us humans. What culture means in its narrowest sense struck me with full force. The lines of the roofs merged from different direc-

tions ... All these things were caught up and encircled by the well-constructed mountain masses. Culture, very lofty and yet self-evident, very naturally – I have no other word. Nature, then, has been reshaped, subjected to mind and spirit, yet it is perfectly simple ... the legacy of a thousand-year-old process in which culture has developed naturally. I do not know where to find the words to express this miracle that is so full of light and that is as self-evident to us when we live in it as the air and the sun".[17]

This feeling of unease described by Guardini and Mies van der Rohe, who during the same period gave numerous talks on the topics discussed by the theologian-philosopher, was a consequence of the feeling that "the old world is perishing"[18] and once again raised the question of whether, "in all that is taking place, a life supported by human nature and fully human work is possible?".[19] For both Guardini, who theorised a reconciliation between opposites achieved by balancing rationality and intuition, and for Mies van der Rohe, who applied his mentor's theses to architecture in order to achieve a "genuine order" that would reconcile life and form (that innovative "open spatial form" that would inaugurate the modern development of a protective but not constrictive space), the theme of life was fundamental.

"Life is what matters" was the phrase used by Mies van der Rohe to conclude an essay on the subject in 1927.[20] Life in a new world governed by the laws of technical progress and economics, in a "new-ness" that "is destructive because it is not under human control",[21] was possible for Guardini, who even went as far as to envisage "buildings in which technology has been given true form",[22] only through total adhesion to science, technology that is "shaped by the inward law of form ... [and] conforms to an inner image " and through the "elaboration of a new order that is related to mankind".[23]

To use Mies van der Rohe's words: "We need not less but more technology. We see in technology the possibility of freeing ourselves ... We do not need less science, but a science that is more spiritual ... All that will only become possible when man asserts himself in objective nature and relates it to himself".[24]

Mies van der Rohe's "skin-and-bones architecture", based on a synthesis of technique and spirituality that overturns the singular, crude version imbued with catholic confessionalism created by Antoni Gaudì, should have helped to overcome the modern subjectivism and materialism in an attempt to attain a new unity that recalled the unity of classic antiquity in form and medieval unity in spirit.

15. Dublin, Merrion Square, 1760–80 • 16. Karl Friedrich Schinkel, Summer pavilion in park of Charlottenburg castle, 1824 • 17. Eric Gunnar Asplund, Woodland Crematorium, Stockholm, 1935–40

The Barcelona Pavilion of 1929 represents the constructed synthesis of these ideas: first and foremost, a solid pedestal as in the Greek temple, then cruciform pillars encased in sheaths of chromium-plated sheet metal which allude to the gothic poly-style pillars and the grooves of a Doric column, while at the same time being indicators of the reference coordinates inside the larger space. The strong wall panels of onyx and vert antique marble create an intentional contrast with the lightness of the structure and the glass walls, affirming the eternal value of time and the natural purity of the materials.

References to human history (the eternity of the pedestal and the materials), innovative technologies and a new sense of space (the free layout of the panels) blend together in a spatial poetry that appears final and has had an enormous influence on modern and contemporary architectural experience. The symbolic and spatial value given to the strong wall panels was echoed, in minimalist architecture, through the use of "low walls" which serve as boundaries to function and vision, as well as being space-forming elements. History and the present, myth and modern spirituality, humanism and technique are blended to achieve the unification and reconciliation of opposites for which Guardini had hoped.

In the Barcelona Pavilion Mies van der Rohe gave tangible expression to the modern possibility of simplicity and naturalness of building observed by his mentor in the peaceful valleys of Brianza.

In a more general climate of resorting to classicism as the foundational moment for the affirmation of eternal values, a number of works by Eric Gunnar Asplund, for example, the Stockholm Cemetery of 1935–40 or the later works by Philip C. Johnson in New Canaan dating from 1935–40 or by Louis Kahn at Fort Worth in 1971, appear to be more heavily weighed down by the same ideal references.

These apparently heterogeneous works share a common reference to a basic compositional syntax which attempts, in a variety of ways, to reconstruct that harmony between the built project and nature or between physical and spiritual data attained by some of its best examples from the classical period.

The common ground shared by K. F. Schinkel's neoclassical work (summer pavilion in the park at Charlottenburg) and that by P.C. Johnson (Boissonas house) in their attempt to re-establish communications with the clear simplicity of classic architecture steeped with Mediterranean references can hardly escape attention.

The classical myth found new substance in Mies van der Rohe and, as was seen ear-

14

lier, continued to feature in architectural developments, including contemporary architecture, posing insistent questions.

The theme is not suppressed in minimalist architecture, as is shown by the frequent references to Greek and Roman architecture (in fact, AG Fronzoni believes that Minimalism was first conceived in Greece).

The natural vocation for understatement, for miniaturising, outside the commonplace intentionality of the generalising type, leads to the supposition that the bourgeois and domestic variations given to the classicist idea in the eighteenth century exert a greater influence on the universe of minimalist architecture than the original aulic models. The imposing peace and silence of the Greek temple were given both a memorial and were adapted to the most modest requirements of everyday life in the quarters of Georgian London. All the houses in Merrion Square, Dublin are built using the same brick material, all have the same classic portal and the same number of floors. However, the coursework of bricks do not match from one house to another, the entrances are different and the heights change imperceptibly. The general unadorned visual unity that gives a uniform appearance to the houses around the green rectangle of the central square alters depending on the point of view and the weather conditions. The embrasures around the windows are painted white and, depending on perspective, play a surprising chromatic role. Atmospheric changes are included in the large geometry of the rectangle drawn by the buildings around the square.

Here is outstanding architectural simplicity, outstanding town-planning simplicity and a simple way of drawing earth and sky closer to the more modest requirements of everyday life.

Perhaps the architecture of simplicity can be recognised in this concept of less is more, in a classic ideal of atemporality, namely far removed from pompous and ideologically exacting moments, as well as being jeopardised by the uses made of the classical repertoire by all the totalitarian regimes this century.

Sheltered from the great philosophical and religious arguments, architectural Minimalism houses the major existentialist themes inside simple and silent buildings in which to appreciate the movement of a ray of light across a wall or the value of a pure and uncontaminated space.

Chekhov asked himself, "What shall I do?", and came up with the only acceptable answer: "Upon my honour and conscience, I don't know". Lucid pragmatism and lay

21. Ludwig Mies van der Rohe, Barcelona Pavilion, 1929 • 22. Ludwig Mies van der Rohe, Farnsworth House, Fox River Valley, Plano, Illinois, 1945–51 • 23. Ludwig Mies van der Rohe, Mountain house

spirituality are among the key features of minimalist ideology. Mies van der Rohe's attempt to give an answer to the concerns of a world weighed down with pointless materialistic burdens, with loss of meaning and a consequent loss signalled by the most significant artistic events of the twentieth century is founded on a search for the essence: the essence of the human condition, the essence of place, the essence of materials, the essence of space, the essence of light.

Only by combining disciplinary aspects with a broader conception and a broader way of feeling could the great architect communicate the constancy and eternal presence in an inarticulate world of those inescapable questions that have always characterised human affairs.

On the other hand, apart from the contingent, required preciousness of the materials, does the presence of onyx and marble partitions in the Barcelona pavilion perhaps not serve as a prelude to the parallelepipeds and bare industrial materials of Minimalism and the disturbing black monolith in *2001, Space Odyssey*? Do these partitions perhaps not have the same function of indicating a limit, like the hedge in Leopardi beyond which lay "interminable spaces", "superhuman silences", "extraordinarily deep quiet"?

Mies van der Rohe's modern project reveals the possibility of a life that, while referred to the forefront of modern technological development, also aspires to a comparison with absolute values. Recently this theme was back in vogue again in the wake of the crisis of modern and postmodern architecture.

A more pessimistic vision and a general climate of growing distrust in a humanist project, which saw technology as being part of future salvation or gradual liberation, have dominated the closing decades of the last century.

"Technology is not man, technology is abstraction and the combination of ideation and human actions at such a level of artfulness that no man and no human group, however specialised, or perhaps precisely on account of their specialisation, can control it completely... even history, seen as time endowed with meaning, loses its significance because the Earth, the theatre of history, becomes unstable through technology, which has the power to abolish the stage on which man has acted out his story".[25]

The apparently excessive and crude affirmations put forward by the philosopher Umberto Galimberti are confirmed, on the other hand, by the tabloid press during the first days of the new millennium which opened with the destruction and the collapse of the most striking symbols of technical and technological power.

for the architect, Merano, 1934 • 24. RICHARD NEUTRA, Kaufmann House, Palm Springs, 1946 • 25. RICHARD NEUTRA, Singleton House, Los Angeles, 1950

The path taken by Mies van der Rohe at a time when the new technocratic set-up was still being formed, now seems to be completely barred.

The possible reconciliation of the opposites imagined earlier by Guardini now seems impracticable faced with the complexity and level of magnitude attained by technocratic prevarication.

Even the formal development of Mies van der Rohe's architecture after the Barcelona pavilion appear to be influenced by the progressive dematerialisation of architecture (project for the architect's own mountain house in South Tyrol, 1934, in which works by Paul Klee and the external panorama are the only apparent physical data, and Farnsworth House (1945–51), in which the built elements undergo an exemplary technical and expressive reduction) rather than a continuation of the dialogue between technology and history that characterised the central years in Berlin: an exception being the new National Gallery in Berlin.

The years of the International Style movement would confirm this trend with the theme of large glazed areas and the gradual formal simplification typical of Richard Neutra's work for example (Moore House in 1952 and Singleton House in 1959). In these and other works the process of stripping down, the need to get down to the bones, coinciding with construction technique alone, cannot prolong that search for the essence of space, light and time that was sparked off with such force by the Barcelona pavilion.

The pure technique induced by these albeit early examples was transformed, in more recent times, into visual ostentation and aggressiveness (among the mega-structures of the Seventies and High-Tech) that were totally immune to any claim that was not exclusively self-affirmative and self-referenced.

A deliberate interruption, a suspension, a pause and a break appear to be the only available instruments that are more efficient for a reconsideration of development, not just in economic or technological terms.

Only the mechanisms of deprivation and reduction can help to eliminate, in a slow and difficult process, the causes of what has now become a widespread and suicidal loss of meaning.

This apparent multiplicity of intents, aspects and research sectors, alleged to represent one of the characteristics of the so-called postmodern condition, may hide a single underlying common denominator: the anxiety arising from the lack of any foundational or legitimating grounds for action.

26. Claude-Nicolas Ledoux, Woodcutter's house, ca.1770–80 • 27. Carl Andre, Cedar Piece, 1959 • 28. Carl Andre, Pyre (element series), 1969–71 • 29. Eduardo Souto de Moura,

Also in the architectural field, it is impossible not to detect an extenuating search for the bombastic, the magniloquent, for visual aggressiveness.

"Based on such uncertain, shaky or non-existent cultural foundations, it has not taken long for the structures of much contemporary architecture to assume either the lugubriously ridiculous appearance of a tragically cheerful, grotesquely uncoordinated Brughelian dance; or to look like a sky-reaching duel between aseptic Towers of Babel in steel, glass and special materials which, by the first storey, have already forgotten the reason for their daring but, at the same time, guilty and ingenuous construction".[26]

This perhaps explains the affirmation made by Claudio Silvestrin: "Rather than deny these works, I question the values that they express, the principles underlying the forms"; [27] and why John Pawson, in a sort of mute cross-examination, confronts his visitors with a series of photos of exasperated and exasperating high-tech or formalistic works before showing them anything else.

A pause in the void of these minimalist interiors may represent, if not the last, at least the first decantation and purification chamber leading to a different experience. As in any initiation or religious rite, the silence and the minimalist vacuum assume partic-

ularly representative roles for a reconsideration of self and the truest and simplest reasons for living.

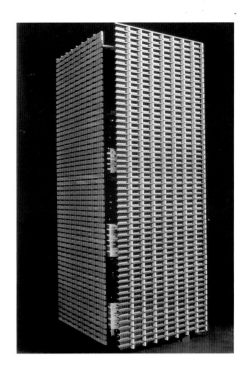

photo of stacks of construction materials • 30. Eduardo Souto de Moura, Cupboard-bar, 1991 • 31. Eduardo Souto de Moura, Burgo project, Oporto, 1991

Minimalism and the architecture of simplicity

In our evolved contemporary world, ever more on the verge of disarticulation, aphasia and a vacuum of meaning, a reconsideration of the idea of simplicity through a task of courageous reduction, but one brimming with echoes, memories of history and culture, sometimes even long gone, might achieve far-reaching effects.

A void of meanings was invoked by the primary structures and the coarse, bare industrial materials used by minimalist artists to spark off a philosophically harsh criticism of artistic processes and to encourage new possibilities of interaction between the work and its audience. Only by clearing the field of all residual customs, memories and consolidated intellectual attitudes that compel or deviate an intact, innocent and immediate perception of things, was it possible to reopen the path leading to a shift in values from inside the work to its exterior, to the spectator and everyday life.

This is one of the links that join the various artistic manifestations grouped together under the minimalist label, irrespective of the methods and expressive forms used: the need to create a mental, spatial and almost atemporal void which allows a break, a pause for reflection, a highly effective standstill to allow a different view of reality.

Minimal simplicity has shown its ability to attract a large number of trends, influences, artistic movements (including artistic Minimalism itself or "Arte Povera" in the Sixties, which seems only to have found its full expression through involvement in disciplines like drama or architecture), successfully rebuilding and developing the whole into a concise form with exemplary clarity and flawless simplicity.

Carl Andre's simple wooden assembly using a joinery format highlights a basic constructive model that is rooted in the history of poor architecture and in Claude-Nicolas Ledoux's "talking architecture" (the woodcutter's house in the *Ville Sociale* in Chaux) and is taken up, for example, by Eduardo Souto de Moura who develops it, underlining its compositional anonymity by enclosing photos of stacks of wood and stone in a unit-bar version and in the Burgo project at Porto in 1991.

This apparently strained historiographic interpretation which relegates the significance of American artistic Minimalism to a pioneering, investigative, exploratory and mental role and assigns its subsequent developments in the field of architec-

32. Carl Andre, Stile (element series), 1960–75 • 33. Herzog & de Meuron, Extension of Ricola factory, Laufen, 1986–91 • 34. Herzog & de Meuron, Frei photographic studio, Weil am Rhein, 1981–82

ture, for example, the role of the first, true signs of the broadening of what was still an embryonic attitude, closed within the restricted circle of avant-garde galleries or enlightened collectors, might, at least, be regarded as one of the ways that led to the recognition and spread of this new sensitivity.

A sensitivity that, owing to its nature and intimate needs, has always peremptorily called for the complicity of a knowing and supportive public, without which the elementary stereometric volumes created by Robert Morris or Donald Judd's basic installations would never have found any legitimate grounds, let alone artistic ones. "Many minimalist works were created in relation to aesthetic legitimacy which would assure them an exhibition venue dedicated to contemporary art. Only an institutional container can guarantee legitimacy to a floor of identical monochrome tiles signed by Carl Andre, or the three-dimensional permutations of the possible combinations of perpendicular axes by Sol Le Witt".[28]

Faced with the increasingly old and decrepit felts by Robert Morris, or on the occasion of the compulsory removal of Richard Serra's rusty plates from the urban settings in which they had been installed, even art collectors repeatedly wondered about the intrinsic value of these works which they had always attempted to

enhance in the only way possible, as an installation and, therefore, a spectacular, theatrical and scenographic, and sometimes even architectonic moment.

Taking this to an extreme, one could almost say that minimalist architecture attracted more derivations from the void and aseptic spaces of American installations than from the actual works of Robert Morris or Donald Judd.

The minimalist work of art calls for a special space in which to be installed, whether a bare art gallery, an anonymous disused warehouse (Donald Judd at Marfa, Texas) or an unspoilt natural setting free from the presence of any other human works. It is no coincidence that, on the site for the house in Capraia, AG Fronzoni's first act was to request the removal of the electric telegraph poles whose presence might have detracted from the place's necessary atemporal dimension.

A void, the absence of any presence that might contaminate an authentic and original act of perception: these are the peremptory requirements of the works by Robert Morris, Donald Judd, Dan Flavin, Carl Andre. As Robert Wilson would have said, a void in which "to listen to the figures".

Having abandoned the pedagogical wishes or fancies of an enlightened origin typical of the Modern Movement and the complete arrogance that guided the experi-

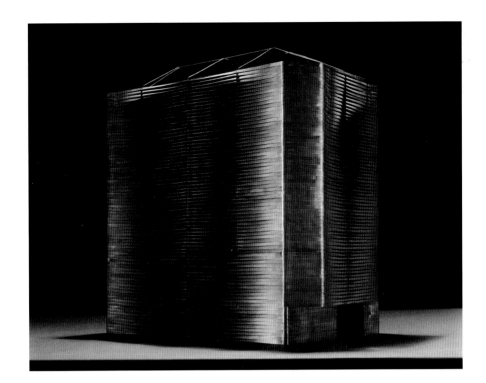 

• 35. HERZOG & DE MEURON, Signal box, Basel, 1988–95 • 36. ADOLF LOOS, Tomb for Max Dvoràk, 1921

ences of the masters between the Wars to lose themselves in that sort of cultural colonialism known as the International Style. Minimalism was ready to undergo tests of greater humility and concreteness.

"The most profound claim of minimalist architecture is its propensity to listen, not to the entire universe, but to a small portion. Through its relationship with the whole, it represents that portion (Cape Rizzuto on Capri for Libera-Malaparte or that precise area of Majorca for Pawson-Silvestrin) in its entirety.

Minimalism reveals the invisible (the great cosmos beyond Giacomo Leopardi's hedge), everything that lies at a depth which words cannot reach.

Listening architectures are architectures of places and they draw strength from the invisible web that is already present in reality but is waiting to be revealed to the light".29

In the practical nature of minimalist architecture, words like light, sky, sun, air, nature, ground, earth, tree and grass lose those connotations typical of business accounting for town-planning projects and that abstract quality that dominated the architectural and town-planning assumptions of proposals during the Modern Movement, which, not by coincidence, were most frequently implemented in coun-

tries with powerful regimes, even if dominated by opposing ideologies, and return in a sort of revelation, to being simultaneously light and that light, sky and that sky, sun and that sun.

The search for the essence and attention to detail progress side by side. An essence that "explains why something is what it is" according to Aristotle, and which is contained in things, in materials, in the profound quality of the preferred natural materials and in the most basic functions (cooking, washing, sleeping) which become conscious rituals.

An attention to detail (the place, the client, the materials) which, with humility or understatement, is strongly pursued by a minimal architecture that knows "how to listen to figures" with a pure and unconstrained eye in order to rediscover how many universal qualities are contained in the simplest and most commonplace objects.

Demonstrative arguments and generalisations are incompatible with minimal sensitivity in search of an equilibrium between matter and spirituality, between physical qualities and abstraction, between the everyday and the absolute.

In the same way that the Greek temple was located in that space in the sky "cut out"

  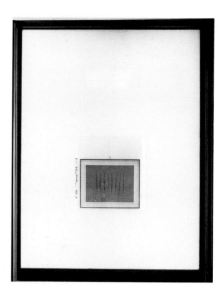

(from *temnere*, and hence *templum*) by the ancient augur, minimalist architectural construction is the substance of a void, its essence made visible and noticeable.

The move made by Luis Barragan, Claudio Silvestrin, Eduardo Souto de Moura, John Pawson and Peter Zumthor away from buildings that were completely open to the outside using large glazed walls, for example, and instead their preference for opaque glass or small openings shows the distance between them and the masters of the Modern Movement, whom they nonetheless respect and admire, and their mathematical, rationalistic and utilitarianist quantification of data leading to a loss of ontological and emotional intensity.

The recognised iconic function of artistic Minimalism made a significant contribution to registering the most visible aspects of minimalist architecture.

The use of primary structures, immunity from all organic contamination, ergonomic indifference, elimination of the superfluous and the search for "timeless" forms allow a perceptive and relational complexity, over and beyond the easy criticisms aimed at many minimalist designs and architecture, and a plurality of functions that exceeds the limits of a design for a "single-dimension man".

Adolf Loos' tomb for Max Dvoràk (1921) is timeless, as are the planks assembled by

Carl Andre and the sides of the Ricola factory (1986–91) or the Frei photographic laboratory (1981–82) by Jacques Herzog and Pierre de Meuron.

The same elementary nature of the composition can be found in the Signalling centre designed by the same architects in Basel between 1988 and 1995. The copper bands of the signal box hide the building and its functions, revealing only a material and an elementary winding technique.

In addition to their precise function, the sturdy, irremovable benches used by Louis Kahn, Claudio Silvestrin, John Pawson and Tadao Ando also fulfil a wider communicative role on the meaning of being, and being in a precise place. Their formal atemporality expands the function and augments and substantiates an everyday moment. This accounts for what is, in practice, a maximalist vocation of architectural Minimalism.

Like the simple stone benches of a medieval monastery, or those at the base of Renaissance buildings, there is a deep sense of values like pause and respite, also as interior values, that are not induced by the use of more comfortable or more ergonomically correct seats.

The elimination of contemporary noise and the search for the essential nature of

things represents one of the principal ways in which minimalist architecture owes most to its artistic predecessor, although it has extended its scope by connecting it with civil life in an action which, if not political, is certainly ethical.

The unease induced by a contemporary condition in which every moment is reduced to its mere material and functional aspects is overcome by reconnecting even the most modest act with vaster entities: no longer history, even everyday history, with myth, as in classical antiquity or in the recurrent periods of classicism (Renaissance, Neoclassicism), but instead with the essence, the miracle, the inexpressible and the unexpressed contained in the simplest facts.

Minimalist architecture: genesis and ideologisations

The long duration of Robert Wilson's theatrical performances, the emptiness typical of his settings, the immaterial but highly effective value of his lighting, and the void that surrounds the basic minimalist artistic works, either in installations or in exhibitions, find an evident ideal consonance over and beyond the mere mechanisms of artistic derivation or consequentiality.

The emptiness itself, the extreme and difficult simplicity that characterises minimalist architecture, in the process of stripping down and reducing the settings to the essential, is radically functional to the aim of shifting values away from the oppressively physical nature of self-referencing architecture to the immateriality of human actions.

As usual the critics have produced three main hypotheses regarding the genesis of the minimalist phenomenon in the sectors of design and architecture that found new substance, above all from the Nineties onwards: Minimalism in opposition to the formalistic excesses of the Eighties, but this hypothesis denies those contributions (Luis

43. Tadao Ando, Naoshima Contemporary Art Museum • 44. Tadao Ando, Nakayama House • 45. Tadao Ando, Koshino House • 46. Eduardo Souto de Moura, Bom Jesus House, Braga, 1989–94 • 47.

Barragan, AG Fronzoni, D. Rams, for example) made well before this date; Minimalism as the outcome of a general economic crisis to which the design companies or those forming part of the world of architectural imagery delegated the task of offering new models of sobriety, simplicity and composure that were more suited to the new phase, but this hypothesis is also open to the same objections; lastly, Minimalism as a periodical return, like a "karst phenomenon" and "constant category of esthetics, always capable of alternating with the esthetics of ornamentation and excess, in a pendular movement that is also influenced by economic fluctuations".[30]

This third hypothesis seems to find the greatest consensus among the critics, once again made stale by an excessive anxiety to classify and catalogue.

While the demand for a *tabula rasa* occurs on several occasions throughout the history of art and architecture, it is still important not to underestimate the particular circumstances, the historic causes and specific aspects. Even the phenomenon of iconoclasm reappears over time in the most widely varying cultures, but we cannot assume that it has a common denominator. The hypothesis of eternal recurrences, both artistic and architectural, is therefore both reductive and simplistic.

Within the framework of a hypothesis of possible consequentiality between the mini-

malist phenomenon in art and that in architecture, a passage by F. Carmagnola emerges with authoritative clarity: "The followers of Democritus, the earliest minimalists, tried to counter the multitude of forms and the emphasis on creativity by reconstructing a world that had never existed, except in the mind – in geometrical black and white. But postmodern Minimalism seems to replace Democritus, poverty with elegant Epicurean poverty, the product of a surfeit of plenty. And the search for voids and differences in the fabric of fullness, to find an equilibrium of things through images".[31]

In view of the numerous attempts made by the critics, above all following in the wake of Mies van der Rohe, to trace philosophical legitimations for a simple and true way of operating, based on pure instantaneous data, it is worth pointing out a number of fundamental discrepancies.

In the works by minimalist artists, nothing wanted to push "beyond the outward appearance of objects and towards a universal symbolisation. Ambitions were set lower: whereas the geometricism of European avant-garde movements was inspired by an idealist and Hegelian conception of history, which regarded the latter as an inevitable and unstoppable progress (the "magnificent and progressive fates" criti-

Eduardo Souto de Moura, Alcanena House, Torres Novas, 1987–92 • 48. Eduardo Souto de Moura, S.E.C.Cultural Centre, Oporto 1981–88

cised by Giacomo Leopardi), minimal geometricism was steeped in the humility of the here and now and Anglo-Saxon empiricism which, through names like Hume, Pierce, Dewey, argued in favour of not overstepping the barrier of immediate experience. Moving further back, it might be possible to speculate descent from the European geometricism of Cartesian rationalism, and even the Thomist and Dominican schools. On the other hand, American geometricism might have been the outcome of the tradition that, having been developed on English soil by philosophers like Roger Bacon and William of Ockham, emphasised the immediate relationship with nature".[32]

The use of conditionals in A. Vettese's text is truly compulsory if we stop to think of Donald Judd's aversion for Thomas Aquinas and all philosophical arrangements ("I didn't feel like starting to think about the order of the universe and the structure of American society"),[33] or Dan Flavin's ideal gratitude to William of Ockham.[34] On the contrary, Mies van der Rohe stigmatised Duns Scotus and William of Ockham, whom he regarded as supporters of a nominalism that led to the break-up of the idea of order which, through Saint Augustine, permeated the modern world from classical thought and Platonic philosophy.

"In the victory of nominalism the victory of a spirit turned toward a so-called 'reality' announces itself, long before it expresses itself in reality. But this spirit is antimedieval and antireligious, much as it is antiplatonic and antimetaphysical". [35]

To Mies van der Rohe, the idea of an order that could offer man a "a totally assured view of the meaning of life" [36] represented the authentic exemplariness of medieval times.

The "healthy condition of that period of society" derived from an "objectively correct sequence of spiritual life and use values... belief and science had not yet split apart". According to Mies van der Rohe, the Renaissance marked the start of a new chapter in human history: "More and more, spiritual life tends toward the will. The act of the autonomous individual becomes ever more important. People study nature. The control of nature became the longing of the period". And again: "The idea of earnings had to lead to isolation. The idea of service leads to community".[37]

The ultimate cause of those problems that "still lie before us today" [38] is this abuse of personal aggrandisement and the unleashing of the will for power (with nominalism and the Renaissance).

As can be seen, the philosophical approach, which is always occasional and superficial in artists and architects perhaps in search of suitably effective phrases that would

support their own *Weltanschauung*, is varied and contradictory and it may not be worthwhile pursuing this line further, except to gather the most evident data and consequences.

Did not this sort of attitude perhaps lead to the unprejudiced and superficial citation, in the contemporary world of art, of single phrases by the philosopher Ludwig Wittgenstein and to the over-estimation of the house that he built for his sister in Vienna between 1926 and 1928? Leaving aside sterile sophisms, the building owes much to the work of A. Loos, who was less well-informed in philosophical terms but much more competent and able to construct a new spatial language and a new architectural iconography.

In resolving a critical approach that now risks running aground on obstacles of an academic nature, it might be useful to recall Eugenio Battisti's methodological exhortation: "The temptation to write history backwards – even art history – evidently becomes stronger as the intimate necessity grows, moving from the consequences to the causes, from the informal to Monet, from Poussin to Giorgione, and so on; bored perhaps by references that, having been put forward countless times, appear only mechanically explanatory in the evolutive scheme into which they have been pigeonholed".[39]

The incontestable registration of an architectural phenomenon dating from the Eighties, and which peaked in the Nineties, dominated by the aspects of research founded on a reduction of the formal and linguistic elements to rigorous essentiality, cannot be eluded. Likewise, the acknowledged, evident and declared contribution made by artistic Minimalism to the enucleation of this trend cannot be denied, although from the outset it demonstrated a complexity that surpasses the limits of its simple derivation from a sole progenitor.

Cistercian monasticism, Zen philosophy, twentieth-century abstraction, rationalism and classicism jointly play a part in the works and writings of the protagonists of minimalist architecture, creating a corpus of antecedents that is clearly not susceptible to organic synthesis. Only at the cost of a strained, antihistorical interpretation could the highly improbable links be created between the episodes, characters and epochs mentioned in John Pawson's work *minimum*.[40]

"The idea of simplicity is a recurring ideal shared by many cultures – all of them looking for a way of life free from the dead weight of an excess of possessions. From Japanese concepts of Zen, to Thoreau's quest for simplicity, minimal living has always offered a sense of liberation, a chance to be in touch with the essence of existence,

chapel, Sumtvig, 1985–88 • 53. MICHAEL GABELLINI, Grant Selwyn Fine Art Gallery • 54. MICHAEL GABELLINI, Wolkowitz apartment, New York, 1998

rather than distracted by the trivial. Clearly simplicity has dimensions to it that go beyond the purely aesthetic: it can be seen as the reflection of some innate, inner quality, or the pursuit of philosophical or literary insight into the nature of harmony, reason, and truth. Simplicity has a moral dimension, implying selflessness and unworldliness". In search of the elements that characterise simplicity, in this volume J. Pawson brings together works from classical antiquity, prehistoric Mexico, ancient Egypt, up to the masters of the Modern Movement and the twentieth century (Le Corbusier, Mies van der Rohe, Louis Kahn), including engineering work, anonymous works and aspects of other arts.

It is almost as if the guiding thread of numerous historiographical exercises aimed at demonstrating an assumption or the finalistic outcome of human affairs, not only in an artistic sense, has been replaced by a more pragmatic awareness of the irreplaceable value of total adhesion to the concreteness of artistic and design commitment in a particular environmental and cultural context, and for concrete clients outside abstract pedagogical or demonstrative intentions. There is no *Telos* in minimalist architecture. The *Hic et nunc* dominates a commitment that disdains excessive and deviating intellectualisms. At this point the contributions may be widely varied in cultural and tem-

poral terms, and their legitimisation can only take place in the name of a sort of elective affinity.

Today's followers of *nobilis semplicitas* discover, almost with amazement, antecedents, moments, individuals who over time and in the most different geographical conditions have used the arts of reduction and expressive clarity, rigorous essentiality and mental purity, elementalism and formal simplicity, albeit in the most varied forms occasioned by history and by specific cultures, as grounds for suggestions in this ancient and modern attempt.

C. Silvestrin: "I built a 12-metre-long bench in the house in Provence… I went with the client to see the archaeological remains of Provençal stone houses. We both entered one of these houses for the first time and the client was speechless because there stood a bench that was eleven or twelve metres long, on the right-hand side just by the entrance. My design was not something new; it was an element from the past, a past that we have unfortunately disregarded".

The Greek temple, the Alhambra in Granada, Louis Kahn, Piet Mondrian, Eric Gunnar Asplund, the palace of Katsura, Donald Judd in Marfa, Texas, Luis Barragan, Adolf Loos, the Pantheon, Hans van der Laan, Hans Wegner, Tadao Ando, the Parthenon, the

55. John Pawson – Claudio Silvestrin, Neuendorf House, Majorca, 1989 • 56. Claudio Silvestrin, Open Cloister Hombroich, Dusseldorf, 1994 • 57. Noirlac Abbey, Bruere-Allichamps (Cher), founded in

Shakers, Villa Malaparte on Capri, the Zen garden, Le Thoronet, Michelozzo at San Marco in Florence rediscover new possibilities for comparison inspired by the idea of simplicity.

The tables designed by AG Fronzoni for the house on Capraia and the volumes used by Luis Barragan and Alberto Campo Baeza are simple. The window by AG Fronzoni for La Polena Gallery in 1965 is simple, and it is no coincidence that John Pawson reused it for the Cannelle shop window in London (1988). The baths and swimming pools by Claudio Silvestrin, John Pawson and Eduardo Souto de Moura are simple and, as in Barragan's work, water is the principal subject, albeit in his minimalist vision: a parallelepiped of water. Simple projects are undertaken by Peter Zumthor and Herzog and de Meuron to recycle traditional construction technologies.

An endless process in search of the countless ways in which the idea of simplicity and a way of being has been and can be declined.

In his lectures, Robert Wilson often recalls the lessons given by Sibyll Moholy-Nagy at the Pratt Institute in New York in the early Sixties: "We were shown slides during Sibyll Moholy-Nagy's lectures on the history of architecture. They consisted of different forms of energy, ranging from a Byzantine mosaic to a prehistoric Sumerian vase and a 1922 telephone. We were bombarded by various kinds of visual information. It was different in the lessons based on verbal information. Therefore, what we felt was not what we saw. And we had to make free associations between what we saw and what we heard. Not necessarily like a collage, but as in a structure. And then there was an exam… and the students were confused and worried because they hadn't been given the answers. The learning process was much longer than a semester, or five semesters or even a five-year course. It was a way of thinking, an experience of associations that spanned an entire lifetime".[41]

In *minimum*, John Pawson makes a choice of images and works, but the book is nonetheless an outline of a research project spanning time and space, which may coincide with the time and space of life, endlessly and constantly used to confront reality and the everyday projects required in view of the vast horizons explored with a free mind.

Rather than the finalistic unwinding of an original reel, the famous guiding thread, we almost seem to be witnessing the opposite: an ongoing process of accretion to the already wound-up skein of thread, in the form of countless other threads of varying lengths, including different coloured threads and chance findings, but nonetheless all compatible with the future woven work in terms of quality, material and millimetric precision.

From the informal to Monet to Raku, and not vice versa.

From Silvestrin to Lucio Fontana to the ray of light in the Cistercian church.

From Pawson to Van der Rohe to the Katsura Imperial Villa.

From AG Fronzoni to Piet Mondrian to the Tuscan Renaissance.

From Ando to Zen philosophy.

From Campo Baeza to Adolf Loos to the Mediterranean tradition.

From Souto de Moura to artistic Minimalism to local tradition.

The architectonic experiences that take shape in isolation and by points in London minimum, in Japan, Mexico, Spain, Portugal, Switzerland and the United States throw new light and accentuate aspects that have traditionally remained on the margins of historiographic custom or relegated to marginal tasks, if not confined to secondary classifications.

One need only consider the recent appraisal of Hans van der Laan's work, the current critical success of Luis Barragan, the rediscovery of AG Fronzoni's work not only in the graphic sector, the reinstatement of Sigurd Lewerentz in the history of modern architecture, an architect who is normally overshadowed by the equally anomalous figure of Eric Gunnar Asplund. Even Adolf Loos, cast for many years as the pioneer of the Modern Movement, a role that was certainly not tailor-made, has resumed his full critical and productive importance, not merely as an element, albeit an essential one, of what had become an unsustainable critical construction.

From a tautologically minimalist point of view, we can finally state that Adolf Loos is Adolf Loos, and so on.

Concreteness and the philosophical influences of weak thought at last allow neglected figures to be reconsidered and a full, rather than partial appreciation, or one limited to those aspects used to demonstrate an historiographic assumption, to be made of architects normally cut out or obliged to recite a more or less important part in a puppet theatre directed by a fanciful producer. The concrete biographical details, the specific nature of the work, the clients, the location and its particular culture once again provide a significant contribution to outlining a different way of interpreting the history of forms. Freedom is again in the air, boundaries between the arts are knocked down, even architectural products from different historical periods can once again dialogue in a panorama that is no longer corrupted by burdensome historiographical or ideological constraints.

29

59. Le Thoronet (Val) abbey, founded in 1136–76 • 60. Santes Creus Abbey, Aiguamurcia, founded in 1150–58 • 61. Claudio Silvestrin, Kornhaus Café, Bern, 1998 • 62. Hans van der Laan, Convent at

Moving backwards:
Romanesque and Cistercian architecture

Romanesque architecture and, in particular, the forms that derived from Saint Bernard's reform of the Cistercian order, are a pivotal reference point for the new architecture of simplicity. This is borne out by the works that C. Silvestrin has dedicated to the subject,[42] J. Pawson's frequent citations of abbeys like Le Thoronet, and the fact that Hans van der Laan himself belonged to the Benedictine order. It should also be noted that the literature on Romanesque architecture has grown considerably over the past years, including a number of widely circulated works, perhaps as a result of a broader awareness of this new sensitivity. [43]

Monastic life and Cistercian architecture, the architecture derived from Saint Bernard's reforms, have had an undoubted influence on all the works by Claudio Silvestrin (Open Cloister Hombroich in Düsseldorf, 1994), Hans Van der Laan, who built St. Benedictusberg Abbey at Vaals in 1956–86, and the convents for the Franciscan nuns at Waasmunster-Roosenberg (1972–75) and for the order of Mary Mother of Jesus in Mariavall-Tomelilla (1987–95), and by John Pawson in the project for the Cistercian

Abbaye Notre-Dame de Sept Fons, currently being built in the Czech Republic. In addition to these examples, as proof of the complete collapse of tired-out ideological and cultural barriers, Cistercian architecture has had a beneficial renewing influence in more ways than one, on Tadao Ando for example: "In my travels as a young man I strolled through the mazelike expanses within the cavernous medieval Christian monasteries belonging to the Cistercian order. Through a myriad of apertures, light pierced the darkness, leaving an impression burned in my mind that I remember clearly to this day. Pervading those solemn and dignified spaces, the light penetrated directly to my soul – a harsh light but at the same time a gentle, mesmerising light". These are the words used by the Japanese architect Tadao Ando to describe the influence of medieval Cistercian architecture on his work at the presentation of *Luis Barragan – The quiet revolution* in 2001. Cistercian architecture, Japan at the crossroads between tradition and innovation, and the influences of popular Mexican architecture found in Luis Barragan the ideal medium for a fertile dialogue.

The antagonism between Cîteaux and Cluny, between the plain, spiritual architecture advocated by Saint Bernard and the rich, opulent architecture of Sigiero, can easily be read as a possible and tangible parallel with our contemporary situation.

According to Georges Duby, "Cistercian ideology, founded on contempt for the world, does not aim to add anything, but rather cuts, cleanses and purges; it is for this profound reason that the construction of Cîteaux is nothing other than a cleansed version of Cluny".[44] The operation of formal cleanliness matched the need for interior cleansing and reflected the real work of reclamation to be undertaken on the land that was still uncultivated, intractable, barren and chaotic; land that the monks would reclaim and tame through the use of ordered crops and settlements. Saint Bernard invented nothing new, but merely returned to the purity of the source.

Also in minimalist architecture, the action of removal is more evident that that of innovation, in a technical and formal sense. The architecture of simplicity uses techniques and available technology, but does not flaunt them, does not make them the centre of its expressive wishes.

Its greatest innovation consists in the total lack of innovation.

Despite this: "More than any other, the Cistercian monastery is a conqueror. Solitary, removed and distant from the roads, surrounded by brambles, rejecting any purely pastoral, educational, theatrical function, it waits like a trap. Having been inspired, the best will allow themselves to be caught. Cîteaux awaits them, Cîteaux attracts them".[45]

Contrary to opinions still prevalent today, the Cistercian monastery was normally closed to the public and even the lay brethren sat apart from the monks in a well-defined area at the back of the church. In some Cistercian churches there is no outside door at all, and the church can only be entered from the monastic complex.

Here again we find analogies with a simple architecture that does not want to assume liberal, social demonstrative tasks, but instead acts as a lighthouse for a sort of contemporary aristocracy who can appreciate and understand the value of this light.

Saint Bernard "showed no concern with changing social structures or monastic customs, or even architectural structures. His focus on the interior person incited his followers to disregard any remodelling of the form: only the core was worthy of attention"[46] and overturns the function of the image of things, architecture and objects. Matter is not the same as it was for Sigiero and the opulent Romanesque architecture with its gold, precious gems and multicoloured frescoes, a path towards the imperceptible, an approach leading from the darkness into the light, but rather is itself, a metaphor, imperfect and obscure at times, but the translation of illumination: "A screen stretched before the flashes of ecstasy".

Luis Barragan's useless white wall at the Drinking Trough Fountain in Las Arboledas has

31

63–68. Hans van der Laan, Saint Benedictusberg Abbey, Vaals, 1956–86

been interpreted as a screen on which to read the changing light and the evocative shadows cast by the swaying branches.

Miracle and enlightenment can be found in the simplest objects. Saint Bernard: "In this mortal body … for an instant the contemplation of truth may take place, at least partially, among us other mortals … but when a ray of divine sun is glimpsed by the soul in ecstasy for a split second, with the rapidity of lightning, the soul somehow creates imaginary representations of worldly objects which correspond to the divine message: these images somehow then envelop the religious splendour of truth in a protective shadow".[47]

Hence, simple architecture is seen as a contemplation of the truth. The simple and precisely built walls are a visible representation of the spiritual and the heavenly: they are the protection against a sense of the immensity of space.

Other ideal analogies include the *Tabula rasa* and the straight line.

"This world is hard, intransigent, harsh, marshy, infected. What better can we do… than reclaim it, and soften it. First of all, by removing all the thorns, gradually reducing the part in shade, the marsh, the swarming serpents… Cistercian art starts by reclaiming, by defining the boundaries, by organising the allotments, the terraces. It starts by creating open spaces".[48] The work could not stop outside the abbey and continued in its architecture: "Thinning out the branches, pruning. The scrolls and the interlacing on the capitals of Moissac are also thickets. To reject them means rooting them out, extending the work of the ploughmen who restore order to the chaos of the forests, order that equates with straight lines … resembling the order of well-tended vineyards… made more productive by pruning, lined up in long straight rows, as straight as the erect body of man, as straight as his soul".[49]

The construction will also be straight: "The straight line dominates the floor, the walls of the nave, the side aisles, the bays of the transept; whereas, the apse and the side apses are dominated by the curve … because like man, who is made of body and soul … and God, made man, the church, which mixes both their images, associates, in balance, the straight line-trajectory of an arrow loosed towards perfection, and the circle of eternal movement, where all change is absorbed… Nowhere, in none of the liturgical buildings invented by Western Christianity, is a more decisive role played by the right angle".[50]

The straight line is used almost exclusively by Luis Barragan, Claudio Silvestrin, John Pawson, AG Fronzoni (in graphics and in architecture), Eduardo Souto de Moura, Alberto Campo Baeza, whereas examples of contaminations can be found in works by Peter

Zumthor and Tadao Ando. The search for the essence, simplicity and silence governed the lives of the medieval monks who followed Saint Bernard and provided the foundations for the architectural structures that give tangible form to these values: the unadorned church, the cloister, a small but at the same time immense square that imprisons all the rhythms of the cosmos, the calculated windows that calibrate the incoming light. Light, a theme much loved by the architecture of simplicity, was obviously divine light for Saint Bernard, but also, more simply, the "light that returns with the footsteps of the night".[51] The light is exalted in the shadows of the bare church where it is welcomed and its changing beams provide a metaphor of time and the absolute.

These themes have not failed to excite contemporary sensitivity which, leaving aside any religious, non-faithful conception of life, has taken the rejection of overwhelming materialism and the search for spirituality as the founding principles of its progress.

Even the concept of Romanesque space as homogeneous, a space in which architecture and sculpture are indissolubly linked, reveals grounds for affinity with the role played by the void in minimalist architecture: "... A relief figure [Romanesque] is now no longer [compared to classical antiquity] a body standing before a wall or in a niche; rather, figure and relief ground are manifestations of one and the same substance. Thus emerges for the first time in Europe an architectural sculpture which is not so much set in or on the building, like the antique metope relief or the carytid, as it is a direct 'efformation' or development of the building material itself". [52]

A oneness and a fullness that are also invoked by contemporary architecture of simplicity as a metaphor for ceasing all antagonism (between light and dark, between matter and space, between architecture and nature, between the individual and the cosmos) and as an embodiment of a sentiment governed by an ideal of timeless calm and peace in which the affirmation of Ego, the tragedy of our time, is overcome within a vaster reality.

Saint Bernard's bequest is summed up in lapidary form in Georges Duby's admirable words at the end of his passionate exegesis on architecture and the Cistercian world: "The seed that was Cîteaux died; it was necessary. Today only the shell remains, which, being perfectly empty, we find all the more moving. Instead we must imagine the admirable curve of Cistercian apses as being filled with future germinations. We must restore to their fecundity those perfect walls whose stones were once joined, almost as if to form the crystal of an ordered universe ... those buildings that are now straight, still bare, in solitude and silence.

33

Let this be the end of the book, but not the end of the search. Saint Bernard".[53]

Saint Bernard left no specific written works on the architecture of the numerous monasteries which, within the space of a few decades, were built in Europe to a precise pattern and with, by and large, expressive uniformity. It was the novelty of a thought that provided the expressive stimuli to that idea of simplicity, translating it into the bare stones of Alcobaça, Casamari, Flaran, Fontenay, Fontfroide, Fountains, Heiligenkreuz, Leoncel, Noirlac, Obazine, Poblet, Pontigny, San Galgano, Santes Creus, Sénanque, Silvacane, Le Thoronet, Valmagne, Zwettl.

From Spain to what is now the Czech Republic, the whole of Europe was pierced by the pinpoints of a new geography: the geography of an idea that, over the following centuries, was enveloped by a silence which only now, outside the bounds of traditional historiographical attention, has made its faint, clear voice heard again.

Moving backwards: immovable furniture

The need for visual and spatial purity in minimalist architecture has other reasons and opportunities for tangency with aspects of history that are no longer regarded as the simple past, incapable of suggesting solutions, indications or alternatives to a contemporary condition deemed to be distorted and unauthentic.

In courses at the Bauhaus, in the statutes of 1921, history was relegated to the bottom of the auxiliary subjects under the title "Lectures on all sectors of art and science from the past and the present" and was programmatically removed from the 1925 syllabus. Now, having overcome operating and ideological barriers that have been widely historicised, it has now been reinstated to make peace and dialogue with a present free from inhibitions and gifted with a greater ability to listen. The complete adhesion of modern society to a mechanistic and technological spirit, a blend of ideologies and parties, has contributed significantly to distorting the vision of a human and social condition based on a privileged scheme and leading to the underestimation or noncomprehension of claims for simplicity imbued with spirituality, as were seen in Mies van der Rohe.

St. Jerome in his study, 1474 • 73. Monastery of S. Antonio in Polesine, Ferrara, 14th–16th cent.

The fact of having re-established a relationship with the ancient formal universe and having reinvested modern architecture with a sense of the volumes, walls and light typical of religious art in the past, provoked, as is well known in the case of Le Corbusier's church at Ronchamp, the harshest criticism, bordering on invective tones, from critics of modernist belief.

Through the discovery of how the theme of simplicity has been tackled and declined throughout the widest variety of periods and places and in search of a constant, which is clearly subject to the religious, cultural and ideological influences of particular moments of history, the architecture of minimal simplicity communicates with the entire history of simple manufactured goods.

A re-analysis of the essential nature of wooden furnishings, unfortunately for the most part now lost, used in the geometric interiors of fourteenth and early fifteenth century Europe may be useful as a means of identifying an additional aspect of this tendency.

Whereas the panorama of contemporary interiors is dominated by an invasion of useful and useless objects which block out all perception of space, and by furniture that is easily removable in the name of a liberal use of space, the furnishings in minimal-

ist architecture are, generally speaking, few in number, heavy and arranged in precise, definite and definitive positions. One need only think of the stone tables and benches in the villa on Majorca by Pawson-Silvestrin, the furnishings by Hans van der Laan, the sofas, chairs and solid wood tables by John Pawson, and the calculated arrangement of chairs by Luis Barragan and Tadao Ando.

The need to design one's own furnishings is widely felt in the minimal area. Movable items aspire to become immovable.

Minimalist architecture is firmly and geometrically positioned inside a broader space of which it still forms part, albeit in a solidified version, and likewise, in a repetition of the operation, on a small scale, the furnishings respect its spirit and form.

The traditional dichotomy between architecture and furnishings is overcome by an approach which gives equal and joint consideration to all aspects that contribute to the new conception of a space devoid of the superfluous but abounding in suggestion. Many pieces of furniture and their relative functions are concealed inside the walls or cleverly disguised, while others have a precise spatial position which enhances and adds meaning even to the most basic domestic necessities.

As in a game of Chinese boxes, the same essential requirements bounce back.

74. Biblioteca Malatestiana, Cesena, 1447–52 • 75. John Pawson, Passenger Lounge for Cathay Pacific airline, Hong Kong, 1998 • 76–77. Claude-Nicolas Ledoux, Hoop workshop, c. 1770–80

Simplicity within simplicity, clarity within clarity, geometry within geometry, space within space.

The desk in the Jewish merchant's shop in Paolo Uccello's altarpiece dedicated to the *Miracle of the Profanation of the Host* (1465), the bedroom depicted by Beato Angelico in the *Triptych of Perugia* illustrating the stories of Saint Nicola (1435), and *Saint Jerome's* study by Antonio da Messina (1474) are just some of the examples that can be cited in support of what might be called a suggestive affinity, if not the filiation between an antique concept of simple, stable and geometrically shaped furnishing and the basic minimalist solutions.

Geometric islands inside similar geometric islands, or, as in the case of John Pawson's passenger lounges and rest rooms for Cathay Pacific at Hong Kong airport in 1998, oases of order and silence amidst the noise and chaos.

It is above all in the field of furnishings that Minimalism reveals its true maximalist aspirations.

In the Jewish merchant's desk depicted by Paolo Uccello, the back of the desk comfortably exceeds the necessary backrest required by the linear bench standing against the wall and is aligned with the shelving at the end, which in turn is linked to

the counter, in a single formal solution that exceeds the simple function of the various elements taken individually.

In the nun's choir at the convent of Sant'Antonio in Polesine in Ferrara, and in the sacristies of Santa Croce and San Miniato, the wooden furnishings which contain and conceal all the necessary accessories are arranged in a space that thereby appears empty and can be used more easily for rituals, consequently enhancing their exaltation.

A lay example that comes to mind is the Malatestiana Library in Cesena, built by Matteo Nuti in 1447–52 using the model of the monastic library at San Marco in Florence. Here, not only are the wooden plutei fixed in a precise arrangement, but so are the books. Scholars, both then and now, must move through the library in a silent and respectful ritual unknown to contemporary commercialisation and consumption. There is a clear affinity between these fixed pieces of furniture and the serene row of tables on a dais by John Pawson in Hong Kong. Claudio Silvestrin's furnishings for Maison B. in Provence (1992), the Barker-Mill apartment in London (1993), the Starkmann offices in Boston (1994) or the Kornhaus Cafè in Bern (1998), for example. Other examples that might be mentioned include: the choir in the Benedictine abbey

at Vaals by Hans Van der Laan (1956–86), or the furnishings for the church of the Sisters of Mary Mother of Jesus at Mariavall-Tomelilla (1978–82) also designed by the latter, and the furniture designed by L. Barragan for the refectory of the Sisters of the Purest Heart of Mary in Mexico City (1954–59).

A few essential pieces of furniture. Straight lines, alignment, order, clarity. Furniture and their functions are firmly welded to the ground. Function and abstraction. Everyday rituals in equally functional spaces. The monastic silence of the refectory is transported into contemporary domestic stillness.

Moving backwards: the classicist heritage

The Parthenon and the Pantheon are cited by minimalist architecture as timeless examples of order, expressive simplicity and extreme formal synthesis.

The classical heritage and the various classicisms that have marked the history of architecture (Renaissance and Neoclassicism *in primis*) all of which called for a break from the immediate past (luxuriant Gothic or Baroque) regarded as being burdened by excessive and gratuitous formalisms identified with the closing moments, however enthralling and brilliant, of epochs destined to decline form part of the baggage of ideological and formal references for the new, simple architecture.

Symmetry, the use of geometric or stereometric compositional elements and extreme formal clarity undoubtedly connote some results of the neoclassical period.

Simple neoclassical regularity, imbued with the enlightenment ideals of the transmissibility and universality of the antique expressive code, is embodied in forms of architecture that deny all relations with the period of history immediately before and are affirmed as autonomous, self-contained entities.

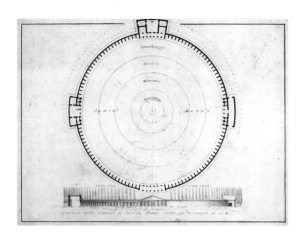 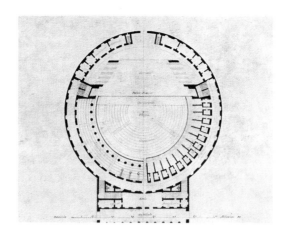 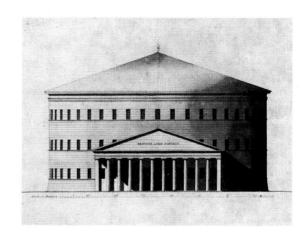

78. Giuseppe Pistocchi, Design for a cemetery, Faenza, 1806 • 79–80. Giuseppe Pistocchi, Design for a theatre, 1810 • 81–82. Eric Gunnar Asplund, Library, Stockholm, 1918–27 • 83. Sesshu

These forms of architecture dialogue with an ideal history (Republican Rome, for example), based on a strong ideological input (the debate regarding the use of the Doric is one of the most evident examples): from David's *Oath of the Horatii* to the Foro Bonaparte in Milan by G. A. Antolini). In the revolutionary climate, the strongly egalitarian pressure of the period was paralleled by a renewed move towards expressive simplicity, the precursor of new developments also in the domestic sense. Without embarking on a complex exegetical exercise to explore the changes that took place in the code over the short space of a few years, it suffices to underline how the forms of the neoclassical code were adapted in revolutionary "talking architecture" to support the intransigent ideals of change characteristic at the turn of the eighteenth century and, successively, to introduce history and myth to a new bourgeois comfort (summer pavilion in the park of Charlottenburg castle by K. F. Schinkel in 1824).
Abbot Lodoli and Francesco Milizia ("niuna cosa si deve mettere in rappresentazione che non sia veramente anche in funzione") open the way, in the Italian panorama, to an architecture that was immune from the subjectivisms and particularisms of the Baroque. The already simple classical architecture was stripped of any remaining ornamentation and successfully used, also in the provinces, for example by Giuseppe Pistocchi.[54] In his Design for a cemetery dating from 1806 in Faenza, a simple circular form encloses a lawn divided into con-

centric circles in which the males were buried on one side, and the females on the other, and within the rings, moving in an orderly manner from the innermost to the outermost, were the youths, the adults and the elderly, according to the data of a probable series. A simple brick wall enclosed the complex surrounded by cypresses. Here were a few, significant elements for an egalitarian architecture, at least in death. In Pistocchi's Project for a theatre of 1810, the equality of the spectators is underlined by the circular form of the complex, connoted, from the outside, by three equal orders of windows aligned with the wall.
In the Stockholm library of 1918–27, Eric Gunnar Asplund reused the cylinder theme to create an unusual reading room where the readers are surrounded by books lit by simple windows which, as in a medieval monastery, throw beams of light against the high, bare walls above the shelves. In the Stockholm Cemetery (1935–40), Asplund created links with history by paving the Via Crucis using the Roman slab system and stripping down the classical temple in the monumental entrance to the Chapel of the Holy Cross to its barest form. The Scandinavian path to rationalism is, on the other hand, permeated by constant references to a good-natured and homely use of classicism emasculated by pregnant communicative requests and understood as tradition and eternal value. The architecture of Claude-Nicolas Ledoux leads to different outcomes, in part, and in some drawings for the *Ville sociale* of

Chaux, namely the wood furnace building and the hoop workshop building, it attains formal solutions that are even closer to minimal simplicity. In the first instance, the building is shaped like a sort of woodstack and, in the second, its façade has an unusual circular form: these are basic primary forms in which no concession is made to historical repertoire.

Even Louis Kahn, in the entrance portico of the Kimbell Art Museum at Fort Worth, Texas (1966–72), for example, dialogued with the classical heritage by proposing an updated version, albeit one imbued with the same ideals of timeless formal value (the simple seat in travertine stone, the neatly planted gardens in front, the portico that acts as an interface between the interior and exterior).

These various neoclassical dreams chase what is perhaps an impossible ideal, a timeless moment of stasis, one that can be reached quietly, sheltered from the contingencies of the present. An attempt was made to oppose the unease prompted by various phenomena (economic, political, social and ideological) over the epochs by taking refuge in this timeless myth. Once this possibility had vanished, there was still the impelling need to defend oneself against the inconsistencies and muddle of a world that was out of step and disturbing. This inheritance has been taken up by minimalist architecture and, from its small ivory tower, it now leads the new eternal battle against disorder, waste, the non-essential.

Moving backwards: *zen*, *shibui* and *ma* philosophy

The essentiality of Japanese architecture and the formal stylisation achieved by its furnishings and accessories profoundly influenced artists and architects from the second half of the eighteenth century onwards.

Without dwelling on the division into periods and a detailed description of the formation of a Japanese style, we need only note how much E.W.Goodwin owed to this eastern culture, in the house for the painter J. Whistler in 1877, and C. R. Mackintosh in his numerous interiors and furnishings marked by an essentiality reminiscent, in part, of delicate Oriental simplicity. But it was not before the Seventies that, having set aside the architectural brutalism of Kenzo Tange, the aggressive mannerisms of J. Sakakura, S. Otani, K. Maekawa and the mega-architecture of A. Isozaki and K. Kikutake, a new generation of architects emerged, headed by Tadao Ando, accompanied by stylists, Y. Miyake, and designers, S. Kuramata, H. Fujii, T. Ito, who abruptly altered the course of modern Japanese architecture. The attention paid to Japanese tradition would alter, as would the references: American minimal art and European architectural rationalism. This unique

39

fusion would lead to exemplary works showing a new sensitivity, less bombastic than the masters of the Sixties, and a new way of interpreting their own tradition.

From the earliest prototypes, namely the interiors in the Soseikan-Yamaguchi house in Takarazuka (1974) and the Azuma House in Osaka (1975), Tadao Ando's architecture represents an example of procedural clarity and extreme formal cleanliness. The use of a single material, reinforced concrete, treated with the care and attention reserved for noble materials, and reminiscent of the simple nudity of traditional architecture, a strong planivolumetric geometrisation, a calculated use of natural light sources and a sophisticated abstraction of the constituent elements are just some of the main features of an architecture destined for numerous repetitions.

"Ando's minimalism is essentially monotonous, repetitive in its use of linguistic instruments. But the monotony is functional to achieving good results in the search for continuity".[55]

Right from these earliest stages, Tadao Ando's architecture would be an international reference point for an architecture that was economic in signs and alien to all forms of visual excess. The growing fortune of Tadao Ando was paralleled by increased attention to the architect's cultural hinterland, *zen* philosophy, the profound spirit of a culture of

"contemplation without objects", empty space and *ma* all formed part of a more general, but often superficial way of feeling and constitute the normal approach used by criticism that was at times too heavily imbued with rhetoric or too engrossed with easy mechanistic matches.

Patrizia Ranzo's interpretation appears to offer a convincing understanding of the phenomenon: "Nothing better (than the Japanese concept of *ma*, an empty space in which phenomena are manifest or an interval between one phenomenon and another) can now express the period in which we live and the idea which inspires many contemporary architectures. This is a moment when the passing of time no longer seems to be linear, but unexpectedly traces an almost circular diagram, retracing its own tracks, returning to some moments of the past, offering spaces and pauses for reflection. A line of thought which ... does not aim to reduce complexity, but rather to search for the prime, absolute idea of architecture in its complete bareness and ambiguity".[56]

As in the European case of the influence exerted by Cistercian architecture on architectural minimalism, it is important to approach the subject critically, with a sufficient dose of disenchantment, to recognise the citation not as the origin of a derivation, but rather an element of more or less extensive support for a contemporary hypothesis and for a

• 88. HERZOG & DE MEURON, Goetz Gallery, Monaco, 1989–92 • 89. LOUIS KAHN, Korman House, Fort Washington, Pennsylvania, 1971–73 • 90. HERZOG & DE MEURON, Goetz Gallery, Monaco, 1989–92

contemporary judgement of a social as well as architectural condition. Even Louis Kahn, in the garden south of the Kimbell Art Museum (1966–72), organised a sort of *zen* garden containing a sculpture by Isamu Noguchi and rationalised the rows of Japanese trees facing the entrance according to Western models. Classicism, academicism, Beaux-Arts and *zen* philosophy were equalised and merged by Louis Kahn in a sort of architectonic syncretism.

It is the contemporary need for order, simplicity and clarity that singles out from history those examples of essentiality for which there is an increasingly urgent need, and on which it can, in some way, throw new light.

Forms and lifestyles from a more or less distant past are explored outside ideologisms and intellectualisms. In Claudio Silvestrin's words: "There was a reaction in modern architecture against the values of the past, and in my opinion this is intellectualism… a space, a cube with a very high ceiling is Jewish, but it is beautiful irrespective of whether it's Jewish or not. Unfortunately, today we continue making these judgements which are judgements of the mind and not the eye. My approach is also a way of seeing the world, without categories and classifications".[57]

Robert Wilson's suggestion of "listening to figures" is at last echoed in the field of archi-

tecture. An architecture that does not barbarically ransack history, like some fringes of the postmodern movement in search of "pieces" with which to build improbable eclectic buildings, but instead, with patience, slowness and imperceptible moves, selects the materials (physical and ideal, old and new) with which to attempt a new way.

In Robert Wilson we also witness the reuse of techniques and gestures from Noh drama, but without any philological intent and only on the basis of basic affinities and common sentiment. Like the experiences of artistic Minimalism, Arte Povera and European rationalism, Noh drama is used by Wilson to extend the expressive possibilities of such complex poetics, although it finds a unifying moment through progressive formal reduction and the use of elemental gestures used to create a renewed form of vision and perception.

The architecture of simplicity did not develop from nothing, it too belongs to history: from the Palace of Katsura to Piet Mondrian, from the modern and oriental evocations present in the works of Louis Kahn (prospect of the Yale Center for British Art in New Haven, 1969–79, and Korman House interior, 1971–73) up to the developments of these intuitions in the work by J. Herzog and P. de Meuron at the Goetz Gallery in Munich, 1989–92.

91–96. Claude Monet, Rouen Cathedral, 1892–94

Moving backwards: Claude Monet and pure vision

The relationship between impressionism and modern architecture has been singled out by a number of historians and critics who, at an interpretative level, are normally guilty of that very superficiality that is adopted as the innate characteristic of works by Claude Monet, Alfred Sisley, Camille Pissarro.

While admitting that, "Only with the coming of Impressionism did the townscape of the new cities receive adequate artistic representation",[58] Leonardo Benevolo is careful to stress that "the intensity and emotional involvement typical of the realists was lacking [in Impressionism], and in its place was a sort of detachment and impassivity", terms whose ethical and expressive value have now been significantly reversed. Moreover, in Leonardo Benevolo's opinion: "Since each shape was reduced to the chromatic elements which made up immediate perception, all interest in the content disappeared, all sentimental associations which might disturb the immediacy of the depiction were renounced, and so was all involvement which went beyond pure contemplation".

Glossing over particularly dated propositions such as "painting can limit itself to reflecting the world, but architecture must set out to change it", and Leonardo Benevolo's finalistic concept of a Pevsnerian-type destiny for modern architecture, for the purposes of this book, it is impossible not to draw attention to the fact that, on the contrary, there may be numerous histories of architecture, and the history of minimalist architecture is also backed by that ideal of a pure and intact perception of phenomena that guides impressionism and Claude Monet's work in particular.

Giulio Carlo Argan sums this up in more open-minded terms: "Over and beyond the rupture with the opposing and complementary poetics of the 'classical' and 'romantic' periods, the problem was to tackle reality without their support, to release the visual sensation from every acquired experience or notion, and from every preordered attitude that might detract from its immediacy, and the pictorial operation from every rule or technical custom that might compromise the result through colours".[59]

And again: "In the visual sensation (impressionist) there is no distinction between objects and space, as between the contents and the container. If the artist wishes to render the visual sensation in its pure state, before it is elaborated and corrected by

the intellect, it is because he feels that the sensation is an authentic experience and the intellectual notion is an unauthentic experience corrupted by prejudices and conventions. Therefore, the sensation is not a datum, but a state of consciousness; moreover, this consciousness is not achieved through experienced acquired and meditated, but through the experience being acquired. It is therefore identified with existence itself". [60]

At this point, it may be useful to recall Claudio Silvestrin's anti-intellectualist argument and the notion of *ma* in Japanese architectural thought, deemed to be influential in the minimalist sphere: space that is not only empty in the physical sense, but above all in a mental sense, and used to experiment actions and the manifestation of phenomena.

The series of paintings dedicated to a single theme, the haystacks or Rouen cathedral, are exemplary of Claude Monet's research.

As in the large canvases dedicated to water and the waterlilies, time and the duration of perception acquire unprecedented value in the history of art.

"It is always the study of refractions, diffractions, reflections and fadings...; a study which, to sum up, aims to separate the image, as an interior fact, from the exteriori-

ty and objectiveness of the thing... you can feel that the façade (of Rouen cathedral) extends beyond the limits of the painting, it leaves our field of vision: therefore, the field of vision does not coincide with the field of consciousness... as a young man, Monet had elaborated and practised a rapid technique to capture in flagrante a perceptive image that could not last more than a few seconds; later, he developed a technique capable of recording and visualising the duration of the impression, its surrender in the long times of psychic existence and not only on the flat, superficial space of the perceptive shock". [61]

Further reflection will be needed on Claude Monet's work, which is still caged inside simplistic interpretative schemes and obscured by the vast, superficial mass consumption of his work. Further reflection will also be needed on the value of his serial paintings which reveal the infinite differences of the simplest reality, which alters and changes imperceptibly and substantially in response to variations in the light and atmospheric conditions, and on the value of a perception that calls for time and duration and, hence, a participation that is almost physical, yet at the same time, part of the inner being.

The anti-intellectualistic value of his work (for the first time ever in the history of art,

97–98. Eric Gunnar Asplund, Woodland Crematorium, Stockholm, 1935–40 • 99–100. Tadao Ando, Chapel on the Water, Tomamu-Hokkaido, 1985–88

the work is not subordinate to ideological programmes, whether of a lay or religious nature, but merely represents itself, like the tree, river and flower repeatedly illustrated) calls for new, more in-depth interpretations.

The pragmatic, tautological minimalist affirmation that states that something is what it is, a cube is a cube, should be flanked by pictorial work which, without any cerebralisms, symbolisms, ideologisations, celebrates the pure reality of things and exalts their authentic perception in an act of vital assent to the simplest and purest data of existence. In practice, this is a difficult path to follow, as is shown by a history of art that immediately returned to reproducing and depicting something other than itself in the phenomenon of post-impressionism.

According to Claude Monet, the miracle takes place in the objects themselves and, to observe it you need only stop and look at a haystack or a cathedral, the object in itself is not important, for a long, long time in order to discover the simple, eternal mysteries of sunlight that sets ablaze and transfigures, freezes, softens and focuses a matter that is infinitely shaped, coloured, scented, in a physical and interior perception, both intact and original, unburdened by cultural filters.

Light and dark, cold and hot (it is no coincidence that, for some time at least, Claude

Monet used to paint immediately outdoors), nature and meteorological conditions (this is not the artist's studio or the museum impregnated with academicism) are pure sensorial data, conveyed using an equally sensorial technique to which Claude Monet entrusts the task of relieving perception and life, serenely accepted, from a tiring and useless burden.

To a much greater extent than Cezanne's heaviness or Cubist intellectualisms, Claude Monet's eye is authoritatively entitled to citizenship within the minimalist stronghold, to whose construction he was well placed to contribute thanks to his novel and original ability to see.

Moreover, leaving aside all anti-urban polemics, the natural environment represents the ideal scenario for an architecture that tends to strip away matter and create a constant dialogue with those inexhaustible sources of imagery: the immensity of the sea or the depth of the sky.

There are few examples of this in the vicissitudes of modern and contemporary architecture. Those that come to mind include the Stockholm Cemetery by Eric Gunnar Asplund of 1935–40 and the Chapel on the Water in Tomamu-Hokkaido by Tadao Ando of 1985–88, where architectural form is diluted by the surrounding nature which

becomes the privileged focal element whose simple magnificence is underlined. A nature which, to a greater extent even than architecture, plays a consolatory role during the most tragic moments of life or those with the strongest expression of religious sentiment.

The continuous resurrection of natural cycles can, alone, be a great harbinger of consolation: the "light that returns with the footsteps of the night" to use the words of Saint Bernard.

The few, simple architectonic elements used by Eric Gunnar Asplund and Tadao Ando measure the march of time and the most subtle changes in light like silent quadrants: they are small but necessary aids that prevent shipwreck in this immensity.

Adolf Loos' Spoken into the Void

It is well known that the solitary architectural and critical works of Adolf Loos were adapted to the Modern Movement at the price of drastic cuts and mutilations, turning him into the figure of an unresolved pioneer, or one relegated to the role of an untimely, marginal proposal, tied to an elitist world that was about to disappear forever and already out of touch with real problems and the requests of a mass technological society.

Moreover, Adolf Loos mainly worked inside a culture and a society, namely Vienna in the early years of the last century, marked by widespread aestheticism.

It is precisely this aestheticism, regarded as an unauthentic and stale approach of formalism, a sort of tattoo covering the bodies of the inhabitants of a city filled by Potemkin-esque facades, which A. Loos opposed with an irony and critical breadth that enabled him to overcome the original scope and identify, in a wider sense, the contradictions of a period whose aftermath we are still experiencing today.

Conscious that his ideas were out of fashion, Adolf Loos entitled his main collections

101. Adolf Loos, Moller House, Vienna, 1928 • 102. Adolf Loos, Muller House, Prague, 1930 • 103. Adolf Loos, Tristan Tzara House, Paris, 1926 • 104. Alvaro Siza, Avelino Duarte House, Ovar,

of essays *Spoken into the Void*, and *Nonetheless*. In addition to the well-known essay on *Ornament and Crime* (1908) which concludes with the words: "Freedom from ornament is a sign of spiritual strength", these collections also include the essay dedicated to *The elimination of furniture* (1924), in which Adolf Loos asks himself: "What must the truly modern architect do? He must build houses in which every item of furniture that cannot be moved must be concealed inside the walls"; and also, again dating from 1908, the essay entitled *The superfluous items* in which, in a polemical debate with the Deutscher Werkbund and the reigning concept of formalism, he reiterated the need for objects and architecture that clearly demonstrated their separateness from artistic intentions and the exposure of an essentiality regarded, in the Art Nouveau climate of the time, as retrograde, a minority proposal, bordering on manifest unpopularity.

"I am preaching to the aristocrat", Adolf Loos affirmed in *Ornament and Crime* and it was precisely an elitist Central European bourgeoisie that would grasp his message and enable him to create his unrivalled architectural designs, like the Moller House in Vienna (1928), the Muller House in Prague (1930) or the house for Tristan Tzara in Paris (1926). The nudity and formal essentiality of Adolf Loos' buildings could only

have been welcomed within a close-knit social circle that did not need any visual ostentation of their own status and, thanks to their culture and sensitivity, could appreciate the purifying stimulus that the Viennese architect gave to domestic architecture.

Even the ostentation of construction techniques is absent, neglected or suppressed in Adolf Loos, and when likened to contemporary works of the Modern Movement this fact certainly resulted in a number of negative comparisons.

But to appreciate the originality of his contribution, and the reasons for his subsequent and contemporary appreciation, we need only emphasise the attention that Adolf Loos pays to the setting in the house for Tristan Tzara, whose basement portion in rough stone echoes the typically Parisian and surrounding theme of the retaining walls for Montmartre hill and the power of formal abstraction achieved in the house for Josephine Baker (1928) in which a number of themes from African culture (strongly contrasting light and dark or zebra skins) are encapsulated in the facing of white and black alternating horizontal stripes.

These aspects are completely absent from the practical expression of a Modern Movement that had severed all relations with the history and culture of the setting,

46

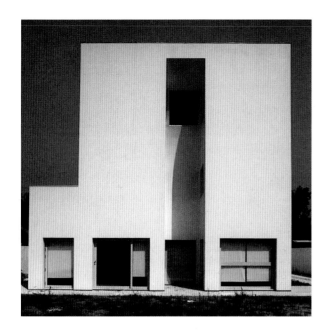 

giving preference to relations with technique and industry which, it was thought, had demiurgic powers to resolve the extensive social problems of a mass society.

The formal silence that denotes the best part of Adolf Loos' architecture corresponds, in practice, to a conscious abstention from the imperatives that dominated the architectural panorama of the period, in other words an abstention from contingencies and from a form of "commitment" that appeared ineluctable.

As in De Chirico's metaphysical work, it was the eternal questions and eternal doubts that shaped his essential architecture, which may well have been addressed to the "aristocrat", certainly not the common man.

Quality of life is repeatedly requested in Adolf Loos' written work; he was "obsessed with immediate sensations as ingredients for a perfect way of life. The quality of smell and of touch, the juxtaposition of textures... All this was foreign to ways of thinking at the time – a fact that is important to bear in mind. Loos followed the ideal of an architecture which could communicate ... with the inhabitant of his buildings ... and beyond him, the passer-by".[62]

According to Adolf Loos, everyday objects, pictures, rugs, furnishings, all belong to life and must be chosen freely over time by the inhabitants, and not, as in the moral tale of the "poor rich man", be designed together, in a single act, down to the most minute detail.

The silent task of drawing our attention back to what is important is the task reserved to architecture, if it merits the name: "When, in a wood we come on a mound, six foot long, three foot wide, heaped up into a pyramid with a spade, then we become serious and something says inside us: someone lies buried here. That is architecture", instead of merely competing with contingencies.

Adolf Loos' white walls and his sharp stereometric volumes, which hide a variability and a shrewdness of volume that boost our perception of space, have survived criticism and misunderstanding, and, at the end of a millennium, now appear to be more firmly grounded than the buildings of his ungrateful opponents, revealing an unexpected freshness that is still pregnant with fertile questions.

Leaving aside the continuing appreciation of his writings, the reappraisal of Adolf Loos' architecture is relatively recent: from Alvaro Siza who reproduced the upper part of the Tzara House with the central niche in the house for Avelino Duarte in Ovar (1981–85), to the larger debt owed by Alberto Campo Baeza, in particular, who specifically cites the house on Michaelplatz in his project for the Bank of Granada in 1992.

Mediterranean simplicities

Recently defined as an archetype that is also architectural: "The Mediterranean… is the void in which things were generated, it is the original place of our cultures. Modernity has always been here, in the capacity to keep different cultures together without standardising them, in the white houses, in the simple complexity of things", [63] the Mediterranean myth was created in practice, in full awareness of its improbability, by a succession of architects (from K. F. Schinkel to J. Hoffmann, and from A. Loos to Le Corbusier) for whom the "poor" architecture, above all along the coastline, prompted them to take up arms, on successive occasions, against academicism or empty formalism. For Carlo Belli and Italian rationalist culture between the wars, a swim in the Mediterranean represented the chance for a salutary discovery: "We discovered their (the houses on Capri) traditional authenticity, and we understood that the perfect Gemütlichkeit of living could only be achieved in the context of geometry". [64]

Long before him, travellers on the Grand Tour during the eighteenth and nineteenth centuries had been captivated by the beauty of an anonymous architecture that was much denser in connotations for contemporary life than the courtly or academic forms. It is to K. F. Schinkel that "we owe the first European revalutation of the oldest, most authentic and elementary Mediterranean architecture of building, which stands out in many ways from the more regal and monumental architecture of Roman magnificence". [65] The summer pavilion built in 1824 in the park of Charlottenburg Castle in Berlin, inspired by the Casino Reale of Chiatamone in Naples, a blend of classicism and poor architecture, is an ideal case in point.

During his Italian journey of 1896, J. Hoffmann drew a series of sketches of the houses on Capri and Anacapri, capturing: "with architectonic sensitivity, in the brilliant clarity of these elementary volumes and in the geometry of some groups of houses, the message of a "concept of building" that "speaks a language open and understandable to everyone" and whose values were founded on "pure simplicity" uncontaminated by artifice". [66] In the text accompanying the sketches, J. Hoffmann comments on the influence this experience had on him: "the picturesquely changeful and lively concept of building with its simplicity, free from artificial overloading with bad decoration, still fits refreshingly into the glowing landscape and speaks a language open and understandable to everyone". [67]

Adolf Loos also travelled frequently in Italy and throughout the Mediterranean basin. His

 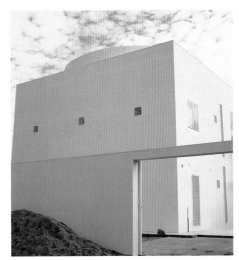 

1982–88 • 110. ALBERTO CAMPO BAEZA, Turegano House, Madrid • 111. ALBERTO CAMPO BAEZA, Turegano House, Madrid, 1988

first trip was to Massa Carrara in 1906 to choose the marble for Kärtner-Bar and on a subsequent journey in 1910 he visited Skyros in search of marble for the facing of the house on the Michaelplatz; others trips followed.

Adolf Loos' frequent visits to the Mediterranean would lead to the projects for the Verdier House in Le Lavandou (1923), the terraced complex built on the Côte d'Azure (1923), the house for the actor Alexander Moissi at the Lido in Venice, dating from the same year, and that for Villa Fleischner in Haifa (1931). Even the Scheu House in Vienna (1912–13) was by no means unaffected by the attraction that the architect felt on his various Italian journeys, as is borne out by the stepped layout which re-evokes the typically Mediterranean pattern of terracing.

In his design for A. Moissi, Adolf Loos combined regulating grids and vernacular features (external stair, terrace with pergola, windows of widely varying sizes) and adjusted the windows depending on the exposition of the façades. "But the most evocative innovation was inside the house where the complex articulation of the Raumplan was lit by the low rays of the sun shining through an oblique slit on the floor of the terrace-solarium".[68]

Volumetric simplicity, clear language, a calculated use of light and the suggestion of low-level floor lighting all make this work a genuine incunabulum of minimalist architecture.

Other examples can be cited in Italy dating from the same period, which owe much to this language of simplicity: the Artist's house and studio of 1933 and the Living room and roof garden from 1936 exhibited at the Sixth Triennale in Milan by Figini and Pollini, and, above all, the exceptional example of the Malaparte House on Capri dating from 1938–44. Whereas the attention paid to poor architecture was extensively and differently motivated to substantiate an Italian path to rationalism or, in the case of Le Corbusier and the C.I.A.M. participants travelling towards Athens in 1933, to search for new constructive rules, the Malaparte house, or "house like me", remains a unique and unrepeatable work unhampered by any demonstrative wish.

Perched on top of Cape Massullo, the most powerful image of the reddish parallelepiped of the building is the anti-perspective stair leading up to the flat roof which is accessible from the building. There are no protective walls on either the stair or the solarium. The perception of the immensity of the sky and the boundlessness of the sea is complete. The sense of physical participation in nature and the weather is exalted. The building is shut into a sort of upturned shell and is difficult to recognise: a timeless architecture, like the surrounding landscape and the examples from which it drew inspiration (the steps of the Greek theatre or those in front of the Church of the Annunziata in Lipari to which Curzio

112-114. Adalberto Libera-Curzio Malaparte, Malaparte House, Capri, 1938–44 • 115. Adalberto Libera, Reception and Congress Palace, Roma E.U.R., 1937–42 • 116. AG Fronzoni, House,

Malaparte seems to have referred). The Malaparte house overcomes history and contingencies, offering itself as a pure means of participating in vaster entities, both physical and metaphysical.

Based on a broader geographical repertoire, the Mediterranean theme was also interpreted by André Lurcat in the group of "studios" at Calvi in 1931 and by Antonio Coderch de Sentmenat and Manuel Valle Vargas in the Ugalde country house from 1950 at Caldetas, near Barcelona.

The attention paid by minimal architecture of simplicity to these examples and to a "timeless" simplicity of construction is clearly apparent in Luis Barragan's work, based on the fundamental attention paid to poor local architecture, mainly Spanish, namely Mediterranean examples, and in works by Claudio Silvestrin (the house on Majorca for which he chose a finish in the same colour as the local earth from which it was made, thereby ending his partnership with John Pawson), Alberto Campo Baeza, AG Fronzoni (the house on the island of Capraia in which the extension to the original volume, a typical spontaneous rural building, was resolved by duplicating the existing block), Eduardo Souto de Moura, not to mention the case of Alvaro Siza who was very attentive to the themes of traditional poor architecture, particularly in his early, strongly innovative out-

put (complex at Quinta da Malagueira in Evora dating from 1977 and Bouca complex in Porto from 1973–77).

"Qu'est-ce la Méditerranée?". To use Fernand Braudels words, it is: "Mille choses à la fois. Non pas un paysage mais d'innombrables paysages. Non pas une mer, mais une succession de mers. Non pas une civilisation, mais des civilisations entassèes les unes sur les autres… C'est tout à la fois s'immerger dans l'archaïsme des mondes insulaires et s'étonner devant l'extreme jeunesse de très vieilles villes, ouvertes à tous les vents de la culture et du profit, et qui, depuis des siècles, surveillent et mangent la mer". [69]

How can we define the Mediterranean nature of design? An attempt, or some say an illusion, to build simply and in harmony, in line with the characteristics and materials of the place and the total lack of superfluity and noise that distract from a full and complete exultation of a generous and comforting nature.

In some aspects, minimalist architecture has recovered the lost meaning of a traditional, poor architecture, one that had slowly evolved over time without the help of architects, and which could affirm a "newness that did not intend to astonish, that was not afraid to repropose 'elementary' models, absolutes of liveableness". [70] Once again, the novelty lay in the total lack of novelty and knowing how to see the obvious.

Island of Capraia, 1974

Abstraction and unease

The representation of abstraction was not only the decisive moment in the development of modern art, but also in twentieth-century architecture. The act of abandoning traditional building typologies, making strongly symbolic use of a colour that was far from functional, like pure white, and reducing the component elements to stark geometric divisions all form part of the heritage of a Modern Movement that, not through coincidence, above all inside the Bauhaus, was in close contact with some of the leading figures of the abstract movement: Wassili Kandinsky, Paul Klee, Johannes Itten. Between the wars, abstraction moved in a number of different ways and, even after the Second World War, further development was expressed through informal art, optical art, the works by Lucio Fontana, Mark Rothko, Robert Wilson and Anish Kapoor, just to mention a few representative names.

Even in minimalist architecture, strong emphasis is placed on the level of abstraction to which individual functions are reduced: note the privileged use of the line and right angles, perspective segments and internal stereometric volumes marked by a sort of

disregard for ergonomic requirements: this produced baths shaped like parallelepipeds and furnishings that were so geometric they could not be used. At best, as in the case of the sofas by John Pawson and Claudio Silvestrin, the geometric, abstract and rigid part of the piece was combined with a soft part, thus guaranteeing a certain level of comfort, and at the same time, triggering off a dual relationship.

The unease experience by minimalist architects when confronted with furniture and furnishings that, by being completely based on certain requirements of the human body have generated an inevitably anthropomorphic series, can be interpreted as the effect of a maximalist need: to meet the requirements for comfort without overindulging them and without losing the appropriate degree of abstraction thought to be indispensable

Even the practice of concealing, mindful of Adolf Loos' teaching, some functions in the thickness of the wall (fitted cupboards) and using low walls to enclose others (kitchens or office tables), or moreover, grouping others inside geometric solids, purifies the vision of a space that attempts to offer itself intact and defined by a few, essential elements.

The request for abstraction in the minimalist space finds a contemporary motive in

51

117. Kᴀꜱɪᴍɪʀ Mᴀʟᴇᴠɪᴄ, Black square on white background, c. 1929 • 118. Jᴏꜱᴇꜰ Aʟʙᴇʀꜱ, Study for Homage to the Square: Beaming, 1963 • 119. Cʀᴀɪɢ Eʟʟᴡᴏᴏᴅ, Hunt House, Malibu, 1955

the call to free ourselves from aesthetic and consumerist superfluity, as Samuel Becket describes in *First Love* : "She said I should have fetched my things. I explained I had no things… I surveyed the room with horror. Such density of furniture defeats imagination".

A context of unease and rejection which is condensed in what Wassily Kandinsky defines as a "subversion of values and the extremely slow abandonment of exteriority and the slow transition to interiority" [71] through a limited use of geometric and essential elements used to build a new vocabulary in which "colour is the note, the eye the hammer that hits it and the soul the instrument with countless strings" in a transition that seamlessly connects sensorial perception and spirituality.

In this sense, the contribution made by W. Worringer back in 1907 was also important, not least owing to its verbal assonances with contemporary minimalist expressions. [72]

Demonstrating the acquisitions made by the newly developing psychoanalytical ideas, Worringer foresaw the possible links between abstraction and the expression of a state of unease: "What are the psychic presuppositions for the urge to abstraction? … Whereas the precondition for the urge to empathy is a happy pantheistic relationship

of confidence between man and the phenomena of the external world; the urge to abstraction is the outcome of a great inner unrest inspired in man by the phenomena of the outside world".

And moreover, the sense of inaneness felt when confronted by the "extended, disconnected, bewildering world of phenomena" (the deception of contemporary quantity) must inevitably result in taking each individual thing "out of its arbitrariness and seeming fortuitousness, of eternalising it by approximation to abstract forms and, in this manner, of finding a point of tranquillity and a refuge from appearances".

Worringer's final thesis reveals a remarkably prefigurative spirit: "… the simple line and its development in purely geometrical regularity was bound to offer the greatest possibility of happiness to the man disquieted by the obscurity and entanglement of phenomena. For here, the last trace of connection with, and dependence on, life has been effaced, here the highest absolute form, the purest abstraction has been achieved… But such abstraction does not make use of any natural object as model… These regular abstract forms are, therefore, the only ones and the highest, in which man can rest in the face of the vast confusion of the world-picture".

The Cistercian monks eradicated the briars and the decorations that hindered per-

• 120. Sigurd Lewerentz, Kiosk in Eastern Cemetery, Malmö, 1969

ception of the essence, and likewise minimalist architecture removes anything that impedes an immediate, simple, intact perception.

Kasimir Malevic, the founder of non-objective abstract art, a movement that is repeatedly linked to artistic Minimalism, was responsible for carrying W. Worringer's intuition one step further: "It is true that we are inflamed by the beauty of the hills, the rivers, and by the golden colours of spring and autumn. But does this mean that all natural phenomena are constructed according to the laws of beauty? Does the sun set according to these principles? Are the edges of the clouds tinged thanks to artistic licence?

Are the hills, valleys and gorges that excite mankind not perhaps the consequence of upheavals and shifts in balance rather than the product of aesthetic laws?

The law of beauty cannot even be found in the artist's work, because he only imposes a new order on what is given". [73]

Malevic's attempt to overcome the objective world in art, albeit still confused and surrounded by an equivocal halo of mysticism, nonetheless marked a decisive turning-point in the history of modern art. It was the precursor of most of the movements that, starting from the end of the Second World War in America, took as their strong point the rejection of reality and a social model whose values were subordinate to appearance, the object and consumerism: from Minimalism to Land Art and Arte Povera.

The significant lack of any reference to reality in Malevic's most famous non-objective painting, the *Black square* of 1913, can be, and already has been correlated with the minimalist void, seen not as a no man's land, but rather a calculated absence of excess form, colour and noise.

New forms of perception and vision can be experimented in this suspension, in this void.

A central theme in Taoist ontology and present in Oriental thought as far back as the *Book of Changes*, the notion of the void also became important for Western thought and, together with that of silence, spread, acquiring further significance and presence, in the architecture of simplicity (Hunt House by Craig Ellwood at Malibu (1955), or the retro of the Flower cloister in the Eastern Cemetery of Malmo by Sigurd Lewerentz (1969), in which the windows take the form of two elemental plates overlying the wall which, having lost all functional connotation, abstractly reflect the colours of the sky), in Robert Wilson's performances and in minimalist architecture. "Space is never empty. The void does not exist ... it is infinite freedom. These precon-

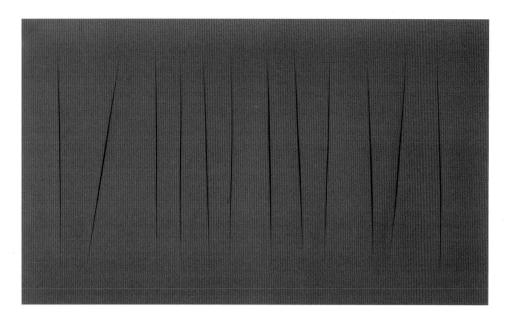 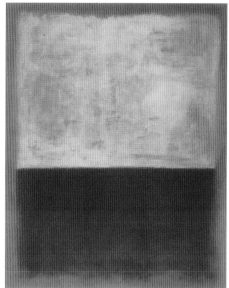 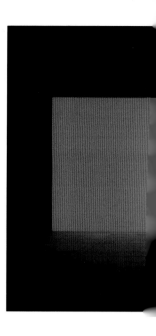

ceived ideas annul all form of perception and judgement. What I attempt to do, what I try to do, is to preserve this space, the void".[74]

Is it not perhaps in silence that we perceive our most imperceptible inner changes and take part in a dialogue unaffected by the academicisms of the spoken word?

"The language of silence is not always perfectly matched by the spoken language. Instead, the language is always repressive, reductive, because it is based on a pre-existing culture that often heavily conditions the process of thought codification … culture represses thought, innocently".[75]

To explore the values of our inner selves and spirituality in silence, and to translate them into a matter that in turn uses what is elaborated in silence as the medium of communication, is one of the great tasks facing the architecture of simplicity.

Claudio Silvestrin's words: "Good architecture makes us silent", recalls the episode when Louis Kahn put off until the following day the long-awaited visit to the architectural complex at the Campo dei Miracoli in Pisa.

Architectural Minimalisms

As occurred in the development of Art Nouveau, today we are witnessing the formation and consolidation of geographical reference points for a particular form of architectural Minimalism, the singling out of leading figures, the varying declination of the same sensitivity and the same climate. The work of formal redemption at the end of the previous century was the outcome of cultures and architects with widely differing connotations and formations (from the Glasgow of C.R. Mackintosh, who expertly blended local traditional architecture with oriental evocations, to the Barcelona of Antoni Gaudì steeped in religious ardour), while today, areas and architects, who are equally independent in ideological and formal terms, contribute to the delineation of an international movement of minimal simplicity, generally speaking with no connections other than a simple, reciprocal knowledge of their respective works.

The visual pollution of the mass media has done much to inflate the term "minimal simplicity", ascribing works and architects to this tendency whose contributions are frequently late arrivals, weighed down by considerable debts (late-rationalists, high-

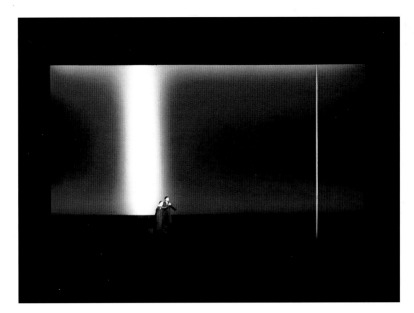

tech, eclectic), or worse still debased by suspect loyalties: a sort of clever professional transformism, which sees in Minimalism a formula to rejuvenate or add substance to its own formal baggage.

The repeated and insistent attention focused on this architectural trend by "glossy" journalism has, on the one hand, resulted in its divulgation and the broader awareness of a phenomenon relegated by trade magazines to the edges of contemporary architectural developments, and, on the other, has prompted the formation of a vulgate that has merely copied its most superficial aspects, those which most easily impress a mass audience constantly in search of images and imagery it can use, without purpose and with no real reason, to establish personal status. [76]

It was not easy to affirm a new minimal simplicity in an architectural world that has adopted aesthetic superfluity or technical exuberance as its standard-bearers: the first steps took the form of small projects for an international clientele whose support has been decisive.

Only in the last few years have architects like Claudio Silvestrin, John Pawson, Alberto Campo Baeza, Peter Zumthor, Eduardo Souto de Moura and Tadao Ando gained sufficient credibility to obtain much larger commissions compared to the occa-

sional refurbishments and small design openings which for many years were the lot of Minimalist architecture.

The isolated and solitary work of nearly twenty years inside small domestic spaces, show-rooms (which nonetheless offered scope for Claudio Silvestrin, John Pawson, Michael Gabellini) and single-family residences for a culturally privileged clientele ready to undergo an unusual operation of stripping down, is starting to win recognition from a broader public and also from organisations and institutions willing to entrust their image to vehicles other than the conventional forms based on formal and structural spectacularism.

A minimalist fashion now exists and is, perhaps, transient.

"You only need to paint a wall white to be called minimalist", affirms Claudio Silvestrin.

The predictable vulgarisation has, if not actually harmed, at least obscured and tamed the attempts that originated from an exercise in regeneration, complex in formation and complete in terms of outcome. Elements, particulars, and construction or finishing details are extrapolated from a sort of total work of art.

Dominant traits among the followers include brevity of acknowledgement, a superfi-

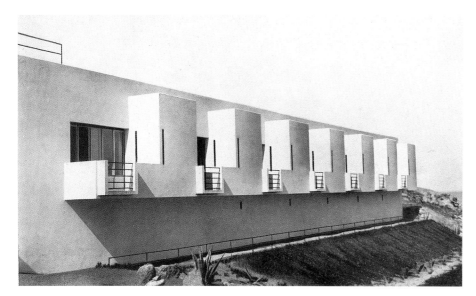

cial lack of attention for the profound nature of the message and an incapacity to control in full and down to the slightest detail the reasons for a choice that is not only formal, but also ethical.

There are no programmatic manifestos for minimal simplicity, only a few written works drafted by a handful of architects for precise occasions.

It is worth recalling the works by Claudio Silvestrin,[77] Alberto Campo Baeza,[78] John Pawson[79] and Tadao Ando.[80]

Adolf Loos addressed the "aristocrat", namely those who knew how to blend architecture and objects with a way of life; by coinciding in full with an anticonventional lifestyle, one that is not bound to prevailing manifestations of status, minimalist architecture can only be the expression of a minority.

Manifestos and declarations of programmatic intentions would be pointless for this architecture that does not aspire to resolve any "major urban and social problems", but which, on the contrary, aspires to bring about a cultural crisis precisely within the model of society that has generated them.

The ability to break free from the vicious circle of an essentially materialistic society, one that oppresses parts of itself in order to consume goods that it does not need or

which, in a sort of perpetual motion, creates the very problems that it attempts to resolve, will only be possible for minimalist architecture through an act of renunciation, calling a halt, backed by an awareness of the value of not doing and not having what now seems self-evident and unquestionable.

Claudio Silvestrin: "There are contents whose architectural form almost represents a logical consequence. They are ethical values but it is important not to turn these philosophical or lifestyle values into a banner, in the sense that they must be expressed in architectural work. What is important is to succeed in expressing this in a subtle manner, through architecture, where things are what they are. Part of my work is to question the conventional aspects of consumerism, or anything else… it's the form that questions convention. Then you decide how to react and what to do".[81]

Tadao Ando: "If, as I believe, architecture ought to contain living spaces conducive to the physical and psychological development of the individual human being, I want to create buildings that reveal indications of human life".[82] "The architectural totality supports the order of daily life; the parts enrich the scenes of daily life and deepen its texture… Spaces of this kind are overlooked in the utilitarian affairs of the everyday and rarely make themselves known. Still, they are capable of stimulating the recol-

da Malagueira, Evora, 1977 • 130. J. A. Coderch de Sentmenat-M. Valle Vargas, Farmhouse, Ugalde, 1950

lection of their own innermost forms and of stimulating new discoveries".[83] John Pawson: "This book (*minimum*) is an attempt to crystallize some thoughts about the notion of simplicity as it can be applied to architecture and art. And beyond that, to discuss simplicity as a way of life, to look at simplicity as a means for ordering and defining the everyday rituals and necessities of existence".[84]

AG Fronzoni: "I detest everything that is superfluous, surplus, redundant, all forms of waste, not only of materials, labour or technology, but moral and ethical waste… Therefore, in my small ivory tower I conduct a silent battle against waste, by attempting to make communicative objects that are free from these superfluities, trying to grasp the essence of objects and to communicate it faithfully to others".[85]

Alberto Campo Baeza: "The Architecture, born of an IDEA, shaped by ESSENTIAL spaces and tensed by LIGHT, allows people to find in it the BEAUTY that only Architecture is capable of offering them. That BEAUTY which is always the final stop on this long journey towards LIBERTY, which is CREATION".[86]

Peter Zumthor: "When I try to identify the aesthetic intentions that motivate me in the process of designing buildings, I realize that my thoughts revolve around themes like place, material, energy, presence, recollection, memories, images, density, atmos-

phere, permanence, and concentration… I like the idea that the house I build contributes to the atmospheric density of a place, a place which its inhabitants and passers-by will remember with pleasure".[87]

For now, the contribution made by Massimo Vignelli appears definitive in the attempt to achieve an overall definition of the minimalist phenomenon in architecture: "Minimalism is not a style, it is an attitude, a way of being. It is a fundamental reaction to noise, visual noise, to disorder and vulgarity. Minimalism is a yearning for the essence of things, not their appearance.

It is a persistent search for purity, the expression of an uncontaminated entity, the search for serenity and for silence, in terms of presence, for the profundity of spaces, space as immensity. Minimalism goes beyond time – it is timeless, it is made from noble, simple materials, it is the immobility of perfection, it represents essence itself, rid of all useless daubs, not bare but completely defined as a whole, in its own being".[88]

A way of being, M. Vignelli affirms. A difficult way of being at this chaotic start to a new millennium, when words like harmony, equilibrium, calm, silence, clarity, spirituality seem to have scarce value.

A way of being in peace with the history of mankind and with all men, satisfied with the few simple things that life can offer but which, if recognised, encapsulate the mystery of the absolute, the sense of miracle.

Minimalist architecture simplifies residential and living spaces and presents them in their essence.

Nature, space, changing light, the immensity of the sky, the changing sea, the warmth of the ground and man's actions, thoughts and sentiments rediscover an unaccustomed breadth and depth.

The concentration of the absolute, its distillation into small, abstract geometric frames (the geometric voids on the theatre backdrops used by Robert Wilson, the water in the straight-edged pools by Claudio Silvestrin, Eduardo Souto de Moura, Luis Barragan, Alberto Campo Baeza, the sky between Tadao Ando's simple walls) reveals immensity in small things.

What is left of built work, a sort of inevitable and insuppressible limit, also of an ontological nature, has the sole purpose of exalting the miracle of existence, nature, objects and phenomena.

Minimalist architecture is contributing to this attempt to bring about pacification with the world and with ourselves, through its ideals of simple life, at the same time aware of its narrowness and its immensity.

Physicality and spirituality, concreteness and abstraction blend in minimal simplicity through the acquisition of few, elemental, basic principles that, before being translated into stone, were assimilated through an emotional, philosophical or religious route.

A way of being.

A way of being that today more than ever before feels the urgency and the need to break out from the endless, stupefying spiral motion that envelops us.

A way of being that, first and foremost, calls for a halt, a pause which is necessary to re-evaluate the situation and what needs to be done; a pause which, in many different ways, has already been needed over the course of history, but which now seems more compulsory than ever.

The countless stage chairs by Robert Wilson, the solid and motionless benches by Claudio Silvestrin, Louis Kahn, John Pawson, Tadao Ando, Luis Barragan, with the rediscovered value of being fixed to the ground, to a particular ground, are the most authentic symbols of this acknowledged need.

• 134. Claudio Silvestrin-John Pawson, Neuendorf House, Majorca, 1989

The need to find, at last, a place in the world where to live and enjoy the extraordinary luxury, the invaluable calm and the extreme pleasure of mysterious and miraculous simple objects with the melancholic awareness of only being able to answer the great questions that our worldly condition has posed and always will pose, with an extremely natural "Upon my honour and conscience, I don't know".

In an imaginary (or real?) dialogue with Bessie Bruce, entitled *CAFÈ CAPUA (Conversation with a pretty American lady)*, Peter Altenberg summed up one of the most important effects of his friend, Adolf Loos' architecture:

"Peter, why is the café designed by my famous husband, architect Loos, called Capua!?"

"How can I explain that!"

(…)

"When the Roman officers stayed too long on Capua –"

"Peter, idiot, what do you mean by stayed too long?!"

"They were staying for too long time –"

"Aha!"

"They were incapable –"

"What do you mean, incapable?!"

"They could no more –"

"Aha!"

"They were incapable of returning to war!"

"What's that got to do with the coffeehouse by my grand Dolf!?"

"Anyone who sits down there, feels so comfortable that they are incapable of going anywhere else!"

"Ah, my Dolf is the greatest architect in the world!"…[89]

Perhaps this conveys what minimal architecture endeavours to achieve.

Franco Bertoni

LUIS BARRAGÁN

AG FRONZONI

TADAO ANDO

CLAUDIO SILVESTRIN

JOHN PAWSON

PETER ZUMTHOR

EDUARDO SOUTO DE MOURA

ALBERTO CAMPO BAEZA

MICHAEL GABELLINI

LUIS BARRAGÁN

Almost unknown to the architectural world, despite the positive opinions expressed by Louis Kahn, who turned to him for a solution to the courtyard at the Salk Institute Laboratories in 1965–66, Josef Albers, Richard Neutra, and a journalist of the calibre of Esther McCoy who became interested in his work as early as 1951, it was not until the major exhibition organised at the Museum of Modern Art in New York by Emilio Ambasz in 1976 that Luis Barragan achieved the international renown which turned him into an authentic architectural case study.

His professional activities were initially characterised by timid variations to traditional Hispanic and Mediterranean architecture, which, in the Thirties and Forties, became more sensitive to European models from the Modern Movement. The real turning point came with his work on the master plan and urban layout for the residential park known as Jardines del Pedregal in 1945–50 and the start of work, in 1947, on the kind of formal laboratory that was to become his own house at number 14, Calle Ramirez in Mexico City.

The majority of Barragan's architectural projects were undertaken when the architect was over fifty and had abandoned the line indicated by the masters of European rationalism, as judged by the trade publications. At this point he opted to become his own client, even to the extent of personally financing some projects and, occasionally, not asking to be paid.

After the Barragan House, which he would continue to alter and where he lived until his death in 1988, the architect completed a series of works, including the Lopez House in 1950, the chapel at Tlalpan in 1953, Galvez House in 1955, the master plans for Las Arboledas (1958–63) and Los Clubes (1961–72) and Gilardi House in 1975–77. These constitute some of the most surprising works of the twentieth century and are the subject of continuing, renewed and increasingly detailed historiographic, critical, exegetic and photographic studies. [90]

Some of his exemplary formal solutions (frameless windows in his house, water-filled tanks at the Drinking Trough fountain and at Tlalpan Chapel, an innovative use of colour, accurately and efficiently simple construction techniques, use of natural materials) or themes (sense of void, silence, a rediscovered need for peace and spirituality) were subject to detailed analysis by architects like Tadao Ando, Alvaro Siza, Claudio Silvestrin, Eduardo Souto de Moura.

The silence, the calm, the sense of time standing still and the profound spirituality of Barragan's later works, as well as representing an extraordinary example of a form of architecture that is entirely immune from all influences other than those of a personal and innermost nature, undoubtedly helped to orient the attempts made by a new generation of Minimalists.

Among the wealth of historical and critical publications dedicated to Barragan's works, the comments by Antonio Fernadéz Alba appear particularly illuminating. In 1974, after he had had a chance to visit the architect, he wrote:

"When I visited Luis Barragan's house in Mexico City … I remember the experience as an encounter with a person who had chosen to put his gifts of sensitivity and talent at the service of architecture. It was his lot to live during a period of architectural decadence, a time when it could be said that architecture as such had been supplanted by self-seeking fantasy, a time when many architects aimed to create buildings for their own glory (…).

Barragan's work, like that of Gunnar Asplund, Sigurd Lewerentz (…), is immune from the commentaries of architectural trade magazines, transcending the merchandising features of the superfluous and the gratuitous. The buildings of Barragan are modest architectural testimonies: their message is contained in their very construction and is legible only to the gaze as innocent as the intuitive sensitivity that created them". [91]

These affirmations are borne out by a few passages from the speech given by Barragan in 1980 when he was awarded the Pritzker Prize. Better than any others, Barragan's words provide an insight into the most profound aspects of his work.

"To my dismay, I have found that an alarming proportion of publications devoted to architecture have banished from their pages the words beauty, inspiration, magic, spellbound, enchantment, as well as the concepts of serenity, silence, intimacy and amazement. All these have nestled in my soul (…)

Religion and myth. It is impossible to understand art and the glory of its history without avowing religious spirituality and the mythical roots that lead us to the very raison d'être of the artistic phenomenon. (…)

Beauty. The invincible difficulty that philosophers have in defining this word's meaning is unequivocal proof of its ineffable mystery (…) Human life deprived of beauty is not worthy of the name.

Silence. In the gardens and homes I have designed, I have always tried to allow for the interior placid murmur of silence, and in my fountains, silence sings.

Solitude. Only in intimate communion with solitude may man find himself. Solitude is good company and my architecture is not for those who fear or shun it.

Serenity is the great true antidote against anguish and fear and today, more than ever, it is the architect's duty to make it a permanent guest in the home, no matter how sumptuous or humble (…).

Joy. How can one forget joy. I believe that a work of art reaches perfection when it conveys silent joy and serenity.

Death. The certainty of death is the spring of action and therefore of life, and in the implicit religious element in the work of art, life triumphs over death (…).

Gardens of silence. In 1941 I created my first garden in Mexico City. I bought a piece of land and decided to create a series of gardens to humanise, without destroying, its magic (…) This memorable epiphany has always been with me, and it is not by chance that from the first garden for which I am responsible, all those since are attempts to capture the echo of the immense lesson to be derived from the aesthetic wisdom of the Spanish Moors.

Fountains. A fountain brings us peace, joy and restful sensuality and reaches the epitome of its very essence when, by its power to bewitch, it stirs dreams of distant worlds. While awake or sleeping, the sweet memories of marvellous fountains have accompanied me throughout life. I recall the fountains of my childhood; the drains of excess water from the dam; the dark ponds in the recess of abandoned orchards (…) the small country springs, quivering mirrors of ancient, giant water-loving trees; and the old aqueducts (…) which from lost horizons hurry their liquid treasure to deliver it with the rainbow ribbons of a waterfall.

Architecture. My architecture is autobiographical (…) Underlying all that I have achieved (…) are the memories of my father's ranch (…) I have always striven to adapt the magic of those remote nostalgic years to the needs of modern living. The lessons to be learnt from the unassuming architecture of the village and provincial towns of my country have been a permanent source of inspiration: their whitewashed walls; the peace in patios and orchards; the colourful streets (…) Being a catholic, I have frequently visited (…) monumental monastic buildings (…) and I have always been deeply moved by the peace and well-being experienced in those uninhabited cloisters and solitary courts. How I have wished that these feelings may leave their mark on my work. (…) We have worked and hope to continue to work inspired by the faith that the aesthetic truth of these ideas will in some measure contribute toward dignifying human existence".

Barragan's words re-echo Chekhov's question concerning the action to be taken, which is impossibly difficult to answer, even in the presence of a strong religious sentiment. A partial answer, the only one, is provided by T. Mann: "Nevertheless, one goes on working, telling stories, giving form to truth, hoping darkly, sometimes almost confidently, that truth and serene form will avail to set free the human spirit and prepare mankind for a better, lovelier, worthier life". [92]

Los Jardines del Pedregal, Piazza delle Fontane, Mexico City, 1945–52.

LUIS BARRAGAN HOUSE-OFFICE, MEXICO CITY, 1947.
The house at number 14, via Ramirez in Mexico City, where the architect lived from this date until his death in 1988, was subject to constant transformations over time and became a sort of laboratory in which Barragan experimented with formal solutions, colours and various layouts of the furnishing elements.
The wooden staircase set into the wall, without a banister, was particularly innovative, as were the low walls which do not interrupt the visual continuity of the ceiling beams; likewise, the window overlooking the garden whose glass is set directly into the wall. The elimination of the frame, reduced to slender cross supports, allows a seamless continuity between interior and exterior. The contact with nature outside is transformed into an entirely interior act of emotional participation, as is underlined by the copy of an abstract painting by J. Albers.

EDUARDO PRIETO LOPEZ HOUSE, JARDINES DEL PEDREGAL, MEXICO CITY, 1948.
Built using stones and rocks from the site, like many other houses by Barragan, the Lopez House is inward-looking, closed to the exterior by a low stone wall. The use of few traditional materials (wooden floors, ceiling beams, simple rough plastered walls) are combined with the devices (low walls that enable a total perception of space and expert volumetric solutions) that have made this building an incunabulum of architectural minimalism.

TLALPAN CHAPEL, MEXICO CITY, 1953–60.
The internal courtyard of the chapel at Tlalpan, regarded by many as the highest point of Barragan's career, is dominated by an enormous cross that emerges from the chapel wall, by the fountain, a parallelepiped of water as in the Drinking Trough Fountain, and the yellow lattice over the entrance to the Transept of the Novices. Few elements, a combination of tradition and modernity, strip away everything that is not necessary from a place of peace.

ANTONIO GALVEZ HOUSE, MEXICO CITY, 1955.
Separated from the adjoining buildings and the street by thick walls, the Galvez house faces onto two courtyards. In the smaller of the two, Barragan has created a sort of inaccessible patio: a low pool of water edged
by the white wall of the house and two high walls coloured shocking pink.
The generous window opening onto the pool dilates the internal space towards the water and receives strongly coloured overhead light that diffuses the room without revealing its origin. Mysticism and a sense of participating in natural events, geometrical exactitude and poetic sensitivity, tradition and modernity reach an essential and original synthesis in the Galvez house.

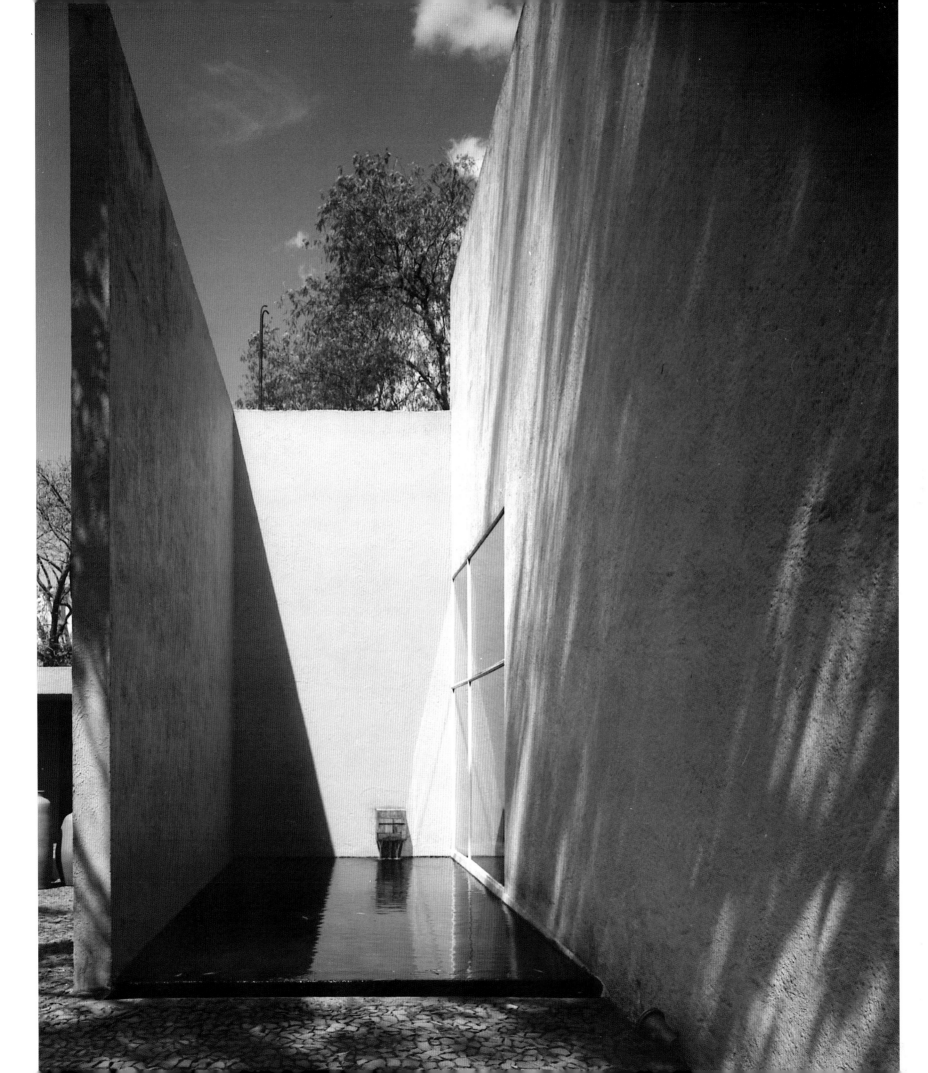

MASTER PLAN FOR LAS ARBOLEDAS, PIAZZA AND DRINK-
ING-TROUGH FOUNTAIN, MEXICO CITY, 1958–63.
"The Drinking Trough Fountain unfolds as we
approach it … revealing an abstract and elegant white wall whose size and location are
quite unnerving. The horizontal wall of water,
always full to overflowing, tenses along the
ground and is held in an evocative blue recep-
tacle where it marks out its own horizon. The
Alhambra, Mies van der Rohe, Mondrian and
the Corrales family house are all here. So
many references and mysterious ambiguities
are suggested by these spaces … This is the
mythical Garden of Eden with its courtyards
and pavilions, with its waterways and pools
… with the sound of silence". (Antonio Ruiz
Barbarín)
Straight lines, stereometric volumes (the parallelepiped of water) and calculated effects of
reflections and registration of light and shadow
(the white wall acts as a screen) are inserted
into the avenue of eucalyptus trees that ends a
riding track. Despite the extreme simplicity of
the theme, Barragan succeeds in including sensations and ample, broadened and learned
emotional participation, creating a "colossal
minimalist sculpture".

MASTER PLAN FOR LOS CLUBES, LOVERS' FOUNTAIN, MEXICO CITY, 1964.

MASTER PLAN FOR LOS CLUBES, BELLTOWER SQUARE AND FOUNTAIN, MEXICO CITY, 1959.

MASTER PLAN FOR LOS CLUBES, FOLKE EGERSTROM HOUSE, MEXICO CITY, 1967–68.
The house and stables designed for the Egerstrom family are set against a theatrical background of pink walls and large pools.
Here, more than in the house itself, we find an exaltation of Barragan's favourite themes: geometry and nature, a sense of mysticism and pantheism, the value of matter and its potential source of abstraction.

MASTER PLAN FOR LOS CLUBES, SERVICE ENTRANCE, MEXICO CITY, 1968.
A high pink wall and a lower, essential building flank the heavy wooden gateway. The road is carefully paved with volcanic stone. The geometric order is diluted by the materials used, resulting in a greater exaltation of the natural elements.

Francisco Gilardi House, Mexico City, 1975–77.

The Gilardi House, undertaken by the architect after his eightieth birthday, stands in a long narrow plot and its two blocks face onto a central courtyard dominated by an existing tree, which Barragan insisted should be preserved.

The tree nearly touches one of the service buildings that shape the composition and are given rhythm by the use of pink and white walls. A long, mystical corridor with natural overhead lighting, producing a soft, almost palpable light that filters down through onyx-coloured glass, leads to the dining room and then, without any clear break, into the pool. The austere dining room contains a table, two chairs and a sideboard. A red wall emerges from inside the pool, leading up to the geometrical, but invisible source of light, colouring the water below. "The column in the middle of the pool goes against all the rules … but it needed to be there in order to bring another colour into the composition," as Barragan himself justified this unusual solution. The dining room-pool undoubtedly represents space and the metaphor of a space in which solid elements dissolve into the liquid state and the latter undergo a further purification process, by blending almost imperceptibly with a light that, thanks to its colour, dematerialises and spiritualises.

AG FRONZONI

AG Fronzoni's contribution to architecture represents a small but remarkably important part of his work as a "designer".

Fronzoni has always rejected any form of critical label and any hypothesis of design that was not total or tormented by narrow disciplinary limits. Following G.C. Argan's maxim that "Anyone who doesn't design, accepts to be designed", Fronzoni coined the term of "projecter" for himself in order to highlight the need for all round design, a multiformat commitment that must coincide with the design of his own life. A master of graphic and formal simplicity (the furniture in the "64" and "Forma zero" series), Fronzoni also pursued an almost impersonal purity, also in his architecture, coupled with an essentiality that, having annulled any echo of the contingent, focuses perception and cognition on abstract primary geometric bases that shape his entire work.

For Fronzoni, expressive economy and economy of means overlap within a project that is deeply marked by ethical and political intentions, and constantly in search of opportunities within real society.

The term minimalism is broadly accepted by Fronzoni who, however, is at pains to stress its broad scope: "Minimalism should not be understood in a reductive sense, but in an open sense. We must take great care not to narrow this term, but instead to amplify it. We need the intelligence to extend it and to stress the richness of this proposal.

Minimalism is not a movement that has emerged from nowhere, but it is still virgin ground.

I believe in Minimalism because it belongs to history. Minimalism was born in Greece and the most reliable references range from Greece to the present, following a very clear path that is far from vague. Moreover, at this nodal point of the argument, Minimalism offers an original contribution of essentiality and integrality".

The strongly ethical slant of each work is underlined in one of his rare interviews: "I was born in Pistoia and I carry within me that rational culture so fundamental to the Renaissance. This explains why I love rationalism in twentieth-century architecture and art. I have studied the works of the greatest artists this century … I have looked at works by Terragni and Mies, but I have also studied the essential and plain architecture of medieval times. By plain, I mean that it uses fewer materials, less technology, at the lowest possible cost. But I have always been fascinated by Japanese essentiality, where everything is eliminated to achieve unfurnished and uncluttered rooms, where only architecture exists and the space conforms to living requirements.

(…) I detest everything that is superfluous, surplus, redundant, all forms of waste, not only of materials, labour or technology, but moral and ethical waste. One of the reasons for today's world crisis is exactly this waste, which happens in every direction, everywhere, in all fields, town-planning, architecture, design, politics, fashion, food, publishing.

(…) These things don't happen by chance and none of us is innocent, we are all responsible or co-responsible. Therefore, in my small ivory tower I conduct a silent battle against waste, by attempting to build communicative objects that are free from these superfluities, trying to grasp the essence of objects and to communicate it faithfully to others. A message, of any kind, must be loyal, correct, essential, it must communicate what is important and is contained in the object.

At all events, I regard form as being extremely important, but I also feel that it must be backed by thought and that geometry must organise its structure. In Plato's school in Athens, there was a sign that read approximately as follows: "School of Philosophy – those who do not study Geometry, do not enter". Form is beauty, someone said that beauty will save man; I don't know if it's true, but I know that I find form useful, not to say indispensable and precious, as a means of sending a message

which is a message of thought". [93] Given that "Minimalism affects the individual", AG Fronzoni has designed graphics, clothes, furniture, objects, furnishings and architecture that, by reducing form and function to their essential components, constantly point to new approaches to a behaviour that tries to be unconditioned by and immune to today's banal standardisation.

Ruedi Baur has effectively summarised Fronzoni's working method in the following words: "To aim at what is essential, to eliminate all superfluous effects, any pointless embellishment, to elaborate a mathematical concept around a fundamental idea, an elemental structure, to avoid waste and excess using any means, to dominate gesture and idea, to neutralise them in an intact space thereby giving them greater emphasis, to use typographical and geometric forms as elements of culture, to have recourse to colour and form only when they are essential to comprehension, to use basic materials, to create the object in relation to its environment, as a social symbol, and to use the notions of movement and time…". [94]

Fronzoni's message, "the only radically minimalist Italian designer" according to Vanni Pasca,[95] was taken up by C. Silvestrin, his pupil at the State Institute of Art in Monza, and also by J. Pawson who used furniture from "series 64", recently remanufactured by Gabellini, to furnish the Calvin Klein store in New York.

Even the singular solution used for the windows of La Polena Gallery in Genoa, in 1965, which only reveals a single work exhibited within, was repeated by J. Pawson and C. Silvestrin for the Cannelle cake shop in London. The austere interiors of La Polena Gallery, Palazzo Balbi in Genoa (1966–67) or the Pernigotti apartment in Milan (1978) have undoubtedly contributed, well ahead of others, to enucleating the development of an architecture of simplicity. The effects of his original contribution still persist.

It is above all in the Chianese House (1967), the house on the island of Capraia (1974–76) and the Walser Museum (1976) that Fronzoni's architectural research reaches some of its highest achievements.

Whereas the geometry and stereometry of the Chianese House are affirmed through the use of a parallelepiped cut along the diagonal, coupled with the successful solution of a roof made from adjustable wooden plates which blend with masterly skill into the surrounding terraced landscape, the geometry of the Walser Museum is found in the pre-existing construction which the building traditions of the Walser population exemplified using a precise wooden module as the base. Even Peter Zumthor did not omit to highlight this construction technique of ancient simplicity in the extension to the Gugalun House in 1990–94 and Sogn Benedetg chapel at Sumtvig in 1985–88.

In the house on the island of Capraia, Fronzoni duplicated an existing farm building, which is used as the daytime living area, by building a parallel copy for the sleeping area. The natural site is not damaged and the two buildings, without an architect, maintain the delicate, timeless balance between the surrounding Mediterranean macchia and a simple building made from local materials. The abstract operation underlying the project is radically minimalist and makes no concession to the picturesque surroundings. The mathematical operation of doubling, making a perfect replica of the original, is an entirely mental operation and "adds nothing to what is there, except what is missing".

The use of local materials, according to a practice whose theory has been developed since Greek antiquity, triggers profound references for a radically modern architecture.

In the Testa loft in Milan (1991) and the Lunanera restaurant in Berceto, completed in the same year, the slits made in the roofs highlight a concept of space based on an absence of boundaries between interior and exterior, as in La Polena Gallery, given that: "There are no interiors, and no exteriors, only space".

Polena Gallery, Genoa, 1965.
The choice of a single exhibition space, free from superstructures, and the linearity of the full-height panels placed in sequence allow works of art to be displayed facing both inwards and outwards, guaranteeing one of AG Fronzoni's basic principles: space must be sovereign in order to convey that "there are no interiors, and no exteriors, only space." The essential nature of the austere office has become exemplary. (L. Gunetti)

PALAZZO BALBI SENAREGA, GENOA, 1966.
In his plans to convert Palazzo Balbi to the offices for the Institute of Art History, AG Fronzoni uses the logic of reconciling opposites. The quality of the monument must be preserved, but it must also express the quality of the Institute's new image.
Old and new blend together. The apparent contrast between the Baroque architecture of the building and the white geometric furnishings resolves into final unity. The ultra-flexible layout guarantees that the life of the Institute can be expressed, in terms of visual communication, within a single location that is open and accessible for all the various functions: lectures, exhibitions, meetings, archives. (L. Gunetti)

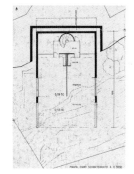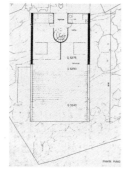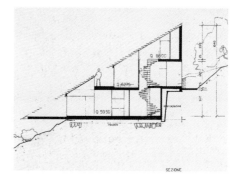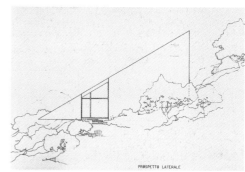

PIANTA PIANO SEMINTERRATO A Q 5990   PIANTA PIANO   SEZIONE   PROSPETTO LATERALE

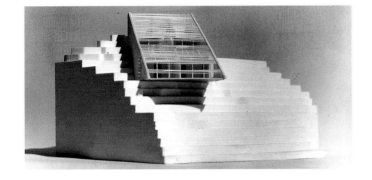 

CHIANESE HOUSE, MONTEROSSO (LA SPEZIA), 1967. NOT BUILT.
The design for the two-family house extends over three levels with symmetric divisions. The design idea is based on a full 3D figure, the parallelepiped, which, when cut diagonally, generates the pitch of the roof and unites the other geometric elements of the structure: the circle is extruded to become the stairwell and the rectangles become floors and partitions.
The roof, which is made entirely from adjustable plates, and the basic geometric shape of the structure led the institutions at the time to reject the project, which was described as "modernist." On the contrary, no recognition was given for its profound sensitivity to the surrounding terraced landscape. (L. Gunetti)

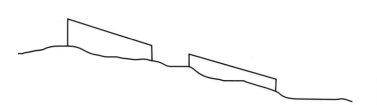

Biagetti House, Isola di Capraia (Livorno), 1974.
This is a project that is extraneous to the traditional house layout which unites the day and night blocks. Here, instead, they are separated into two distinct segments by duplicating the existing building volume, an old shelter used by local shepherds.
The whole is designed, both externally and internally, using modular and linear elements that organise the space. The simplicity of all the furnishing components on the one hand renders the function explicit (as in the case of the tables, beds and the kitchen block), and on the other, conceals a complex subdivision of the interiors based on function as in the fitted cupboards.
Fronzoni's capacity to make the architecture of interiors open to spatiality, by using walls that double as partitions and containers, enables him to hide all the necessary accessories and at the same time create fitted rooms. (L. Gunetti)

DESIGN FOR FURNITURE STORE, MILAN, 1976.
The store was furnished using the furniture on sale: furnishings from the series '64 by Fronzoni himself. In addition to the abolition of parapets and banisters on the upper floor, his use of frameless windows on the external façade marks a significant anticipation. (L. Gunetti)

WALSER MUSEUM, ALAGNA VALSESIA, 1976.
Separated from the pre-existing building, which is completely transparent, given that emphasis is placed on the architectural quality of the Walser house, organised in relation to a geometric grid based on the square module, Fronzoni's contribution provides the ideal support for the furnishings, working implements and clothes that illustrate the community's life "project." (L. Gunetti)

LEONARDI APARTMENT, GENOA, 1979.
By eliminating the non-structural elements of the five pre-existing rooms, Fronzoni creates an open, dynamic space that is used to define just two areas. The day-night areas, comprising a large multipurpose room whose furnishings, all designed by Fronzoni, are positioned in the centre, and a service area. Only two colours are used: white for the walls and black for the floors paved in Ligurian slate. (L. Gunetti)

PERNIGOTTI APARTMENT, MILAN, 1978.
In the refurbishment project for a small apartment measuring just 62 square metres, Fronzoni adopts a module marker that is developed on different scales to fit different dimensions: the wall in glass blocks used to separate the bedroom area from the living area, the square motifs on the floor, the fitted partitions, the furnishings from series '64.
Space is once again sovereign, even on this occasion when geometry gives abstract form and uniformity to the different functions. (L. Gunetti)

Installations for ' Arte e Città' , Genoa, 1979–81.
The various exhibitions designed and installed at Genoa by Fronzoni as part of the "Arte e Città" events were held in different venues. Hence, the decision to design three display systems that would be different and autonomous from the pre-existing architectural structures, as well as being flexible and easy to move. The first consists of modular parallelepipeds drawn in axonometry, the second is a self-bearing plane at a slant of 60 degrees; the third, for sculptures, is a parallelepiped in clear polymethylmetacrylate, open on two sides.
The changing layout of these simple geometric elements has allowed a wide variety of works to be displayed, always creating an original and new sense of space. (L. Gunetti)

TESTA LOFT, MILAN, 1991.
How can a clear solution to the inside-outside relationship be obtained in an industrial building: Fronzoni shows this by creating two glass walls on the short sides of the rectangular structure. The large glass wall on the end wall continues up to the roof and skylight to join the rear glass wall on the mezzanine-bedroom area.
The entire service and bedroom area is split onto two levels linked by an essential wooden stair, closed by sliding panels and white cupboards. The mezzanine contains a functional cupboard block which provides the necessary closed space to give greater privacy to the bedroom. (L. Gunetti)

PERSONAL EXHIBITION ' PROGETTARE VOCE DEL VERBO AMARE' , SPAZIO CALDERARA, MILAN, 2001.
A single sloping plane gives movement to the space and, at the same time, reveals the provisional nature of the event. Graphic works are placed around the edge of the room and, on the plane, the furnishings and design items, once again declaring that a lifetime's research can be kept in balance on the "sloping plane" of design. (L. Gunetti)

TADAO ANDO

Tadao Ando's vast, and some say repetitive and monotonous architectural output commences with a first, exemplary and definitive prototype, namely the Azuma House in Osaka of 1975. After spending several years in the West, from which he drew inspiration and elemental constructive and philosophical knowledge (ranging from the Cistercian abbeys to the Camposanto in Pisa, from the masterpieces of the Modern Movement to minimalist art), Ando fuses ancient and modern Western requests for simplicity with a refined and innovative interpretation of the values of ancient Japanese architecture.

Having announced that the formal brutalist repertoire of Japanese architecture during the Sixties was obsolete, although echoes still remain in his early works, like the Hiraoka House or Shibata house of 1972, and accepting the confrontation with disorder, crowdedness and convulsion that are particularly true of modern Japanese cities, Ando undertakes a silent battle against superfluity and aesthetic noise. This battle, although motivated by precise circumstances and connoted by evident debts to national tradition, has the strength and authority to become an exemplary and absolute proposal.

Ando's international success testifies to the success of his attempt.

In Azuma house the architect introduces those materials, compositional elements, spatial solutions and attention to detail which would become typical of all his later productions.

Solid walls in reinforced concrete insulate and protect a centripetal architecture that is completely enclosed. There is no dialogue whatsoever with the disordered surroundings; Azuma House, like much of Ando's architecture, has no openings, windows or views outside, barring those that are strictly necessary. Light and air come exclusively from the inner court where, as in medieval cloisters, you can watch the fascinating and constantly changing sky.

The formal abstraction of the façade, a bare concrete wall slit by the rectangle of the entrance, is mitigated by an expert use of material: not the béton brut, but a sensitive use of reinforced concrete that reveals the marks of the formwork fixings and the supports for the reinforcing rods. One aspect that is barely mentioned by observers of Ando's work is that the light geometric pattern, a mixture of squares and dots, is not rigid, but traces slight curves and bends caused, as in Raku ceramics, by the expected but not entirely controllable margin of uncertainty required by the material in its transformation from an almost liquid substance into the solid state. It almost looks as if the formworks have given way or become pliant under the thrust of gradual additions of concrete.

Ando uses concrete as a contemporary and abstract material but, at the same time, recovers those processes, a blend of artifice and naturalness, that were the unmistakable register of an Oriental tradition pervaded by subtle forms of tension.

The solid concrete walls house all the systems and technological installations, with no possibility of on-site variations, using a process of planning and foresight that is unusual in contemporary architecture. The resulting simplicity is the product of calculated complexity and this also accounts for the long lead times required to plan and complete each of Ando's works.

The Azuma house, which is peremptorily closed to the outside, only looks in on itself, into its central void where only natural elements untouched by man's presence can be seen.

A silence and a timeless calm pervade the terse settings set aside for everyday rituals, making no concessions to the needs of contemporary comfort. This is amply borne out by the fact that you can only move from the first volume on the street to the second by passing through the uncovered area in the small courtyard (as in AG Fronzoni's house on the island of Capraia), and likewise the bathroom can only be reached from the pantry-kitchen area.

Ando's houses probably offer the extreme luxury of rejecting a standardised way of life and choosing to accept a self-imposed discipline "which enforces reflection about real values and the experience of many realities: heat, cold, sun, rain, wind, snow, light, dark and the infinite gradations and nuances which life creates between such extremes".[96]

"Today, the major task is building walls that cut the interior off entirely from the exterior. In this process, the ambiguity of the wall, which is simultaneously interior and exterior is of the greatest significance. I employ walls to delineate a space that is physically and psychologically isolated from the outside world ... [In the Matsumoto House, for example,] walls which stand independently in the world of nature delineate a territory for human habitation. Inexpressive in themselves, the two major boundary walls are protective devices for the interior. At the same time they reflect the changes taking place in the natural world and help to introduce it into the daily lives of the inhabitants. The limiting operation of the walls directly reveals the boldness of the house itself".[97]

"I try to use a modern material – concrete and, specifically, concrete walls – in simplified forms to realize a kind of space that is possible because I am Japanese. This rests on a simple aesthetic awareness cultivated in me as a Japanese person. It seems to me that, at present, concrete is the most suitable material for realizing spaces created by rays of sunlight. But the concrete I employ does not have plastic rigidity or weight. Instead, it must be homogeneous and light and must create surfaces. When they agree with my aesthetic image, walls become abstract, are negated, and approach the ultimate limit of space. Their actuality is lost, and only the space they enclose gives a sense of really existing. Under these conditions, volume and projected light alone float into prominence as hints of the spatial composition".[98]

The sense of being in a place is of great value to Ando, within the constant, magmatic and extremely rapid daily movements of the whole of modern Japanese society.

Light, shadow, calm and silence surround this attempt, albeit still pervaded by subtle questions and concerns, to attain this difficult condition of tranquillity, to build places in which man can live poetically.

The prevailing interpretation of Ando's architecture as the expression of a happy relationship with nature and as a renewed occasion to experiment interior values was recently corrected by F. Dal Co on a number of interesting points: "The architectural poetics of Ando "the minimalist" is supposed to be able to resolve the conflict between earth and world, no less... Obviously, these critics find it impossible to say anything at all about the complex and contradictory meanings which make up the very nerve-system of Ando's so-called minimalist architectural language: the intertwined truths and sleights of hand, the conciseness and the echoing allusiveness, the occasional gravity and the frequent severity, the fastidiousness and (at times) the imprecision ... In the middle of all this Ando, just occasionally ... hits on something that reaches the very highest level of serious and tragic discourse, crossing the line beyond which there is nothing but life itself, in all its emptiness".[99]

Ando's spatial and structural nudism, with its grey corollaries due to the exclusive use of concrete, may be read as a disenchanted reflection on mankind's "miserable" condition, but cannot escape his conscious commitment to an architecture that must "contain living spaces conducive to the physical and psychological development of the individual human being ... create buildings that reveal indications of human life".[100]

Faced with opinions, albeit authoritative, like that of F. Dal Co, we prefer to withhold judgement and rely on the more comfortable words of Ando himself, in the awareness that the path to simplicity, although not impossible, is undoubtedly difficult: "On the surface, my architecture may look like abstract space trimmed of all humanity and function, and any other aspect of daily life. This is because the spaces in my work are naked. I am not attempting to produce spatial abstractions, but spatial prototypes. My spaces are the emotional expression of various people rather than an intellectual operation ... I call this spatial prototype the "emotionally fundamental space". Once it has been created, I follow this procedure to sublimate it into a symbolic space (...). I am aiming for architecture that symbolises and includes spaces for modern daily life".[101]

Azuma House, Osaka, 1975.
"This small house was the point of departure for my subsequent work. It is a memorable building for me, one of which I am very fond.
In the central part of Osaka, the wooden buildings that survived the war can still be spotted. The Row House in Sumiyoshi, for example, replaced the middle portion of three such wooden row houses. My intention was to insert a concrete box and to create within a microcosm. A simple composition but with the deserved spaces, closed but dramatized by light – such was the image I sought to develop.
The spatial organisation is centripetal with a courtyard occupying the middle portion of the tripartite plan. This courtyard is the center of everyday life and at times the center of imaginative life. Each room is entered from the courtyard. On the first floor, the courtyard is flanked by the living room on one side and the kitchen, the dining room and the bathroom on the other. On the upper level, the courtyard separates the master bedroom from the children's room. By means of this composition the courtyard assures privacy for all four rooms.
The house completely closes itself off from the street. Light from the sky enters the opening and illuminates the entrance. The light which is reflected onto the street by the vertical and horizontal planes of the recess acts as the mediator in relating the inward-looking house to the street". (T. Ando)

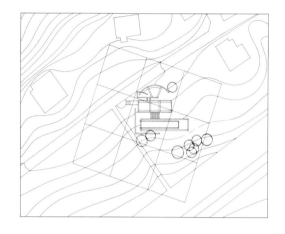  

Casa Koshino, Ashiya, Hyogo, 1979–80

"Two inorganic concrete boxes, arranged in parallel so as to avoid scattered trees, are half-buried in the verdant slope of a national park. The building, though autonomous, obeys the logic of nature. The two boxes of different size are linked by an underground corridor and also flank a courtyard.

One volume contains two levels; the lower level accomodating a double-height living room, the kitchen and dining room, while the master bedroom is on the upper level. The other volume houses six rooms for children as well as a tatami room, all in a row, and includes a lobby and a bathroom.

The smoothly finished, stepped courtyard generated between the two volumes suggests a fabric placed over the sloping contour of the site. In other words, the stepping of the courtyard is symbolic of the intrinsic nature of the site.

The slits, cut in orderly fashion into the walls facing the courtyard, are an apparatus for generating diverse intersections of light and shadow". (T. Ando)

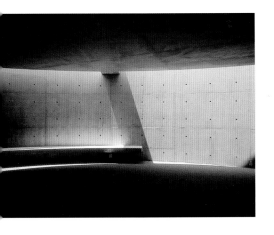  

KIDOSAKI HOUSE, TOKYO, 1982–85.
"Located in a deluxe residential suburb of Tokyo, this is a three-family house designed for an architect and his wife, and their parents. Borrowing in concept from multi-unit housing, the house affords the occupants privacy in their living quarters and companionship in their daily activities. The building consists of a cubic volume and a protective wall along the property line that ends in a quarter-circle arc. This arc curves inward from the gentle slope of the front street, and guides visitors into the house. Courtyards and terraces are arranged on various levels in the building, and these exterior spaces introduce the experience of light, wind, and rain into daily living while serving to connect the living quarters of the three families.
In the northern front garden and southern courtyard I have planted the same variety of tree as formerly grew on the site, wishing to maintain continuity in the memory of the owners and in the memory of the land as a place. From the simple composition of this house emerges a complex, labyrinthine space for the varied lifestyles of the three families". (T. Ando)

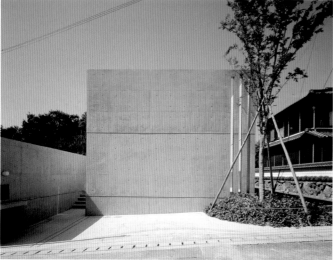

Nakayama House, Suzaku-nara, 1983–85.
"The Nakayama House is located in a residential area that is being developed on the border of Nara and Kyoto prefectures. I have placed in this landscape a concrete rectangular prism, with a plan 7 meters by 19 meters and a height of two stories. The building is divided along its length in two, with one half being given over to a courtyard and the other to the living spaces. On the first floor are the dining room and the living room; on the second floor are the bedroom, a Japanese style room, and a terrace which takes up half the floor area. This terrace in linked by an open stairway with the first-floor courtyard and is part of a three-dimensional outdoor space.
One enters the building by way of a narrow passageway squeezed between the building and a wall along the property line. The outdoor landscape is completely shut out. I deliberately chose to use a single material for the whole composition in order to purify the character of the space. Each room opens out on the courtyard and faces the wall opposite, thus becoming a part of the courtyard". (T. Ando)

Chapel on Mount Rokko, Kobe, 1985.
"This small church is located on a verdant slope near the summit of 1000-meter Mt. Rokko. It consists of a chapel and bell tower, a covered colonnade, and free standing garden wall that articulates a portion of the landscape. The colonnade, which transports visitors from the everyday to the sacred realm of the chapel, is enclosed in frosted glass walls. The far end of the colonnade is open and frames a spectacular vista of forest and distant ocean. Sunlight is softened in passing through the frosted glass, and thus filtered, evenly fills the long, slender space of the colonnade.

After passing through the soft, suspended ambience of the colonnade, visitors enter the chapel where, in contrast, light is rendered as sharply directional. The chapel's theme is progression through shadow and light — the contrast of light and darkness. A post and beam form an inverted cross in dividing a large window on the left; intercepting the sunlight, they cast a distinct cruciform shadow on the floor. This monochromatic space, restricted in its materials to concrete, stone, steel, and glass, draws the exterior greenery inside to become an interior scenery, and underscores nature's depth". (T. Ando)

CHURCH OF LIGHT, IBARAKI, 1987–88.

"This church is located in a quiet residential suburb of Osaka. It consists of a rectangular volume sliced through at a fifteen-degree angle by a completely free standing wall that separates the entrance from the chapel. Light penetrates the profound darkness of this box through a cross which is cut out of the altar wall. The floor and pews are made of rough scaffolding planks, which are low cost and also ultimately suited to the character of the space. I have always used natural materials for parts of a building that come into contact with people's hands or feet, as I am convinced that materials having substance, such as wood or concrete, are invaluable for building, and that it is essentially through our senses that we become aware of architecture.

Openings have been limited in this space, for light shows its brilliance only against a backdrop of darkness. Nature's presence is also limited to the element of light and is rendered exceedingly abstract. In responding to such an abstraction, the architecture grows continually purer. The linear pattern formed on the floor by rays from the sun and a migrating cross of light expresses with purity man's relationship with nature". (T. Ando)

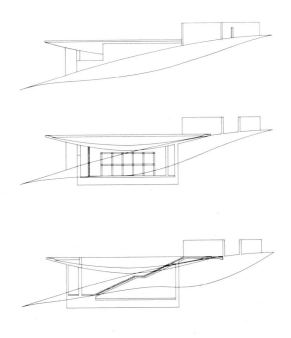

TEMPLE OF WATER, AWAJISHIMA, 1989–90.

"Hompukuji – a temple of the Shingon sect, is located on an island in Japan's Inland Sea. This project is for a new main hall, Mizumido, and has its site above the existing compound on a hill that affords a sweeping view of Osaka Bay. Instead of the massive roof symbolic of Buddhist temples, I have given Mizumido living lotus plants for its symbol. I wanted to create a hall whose entrance would part the surface of a pond filled with green lotus plants and seem to draw visitors under the water. The oval pond, 40 meters long and 30 meters wide, is placed on a small bluff and the main hall itself is located underground beneath it. In composition, the hall is a square room contained in a round room. Pillars four meters high line up in the hall at intervals of one ken (a ken is a traditional Japanese module equivalent to 1.8 meters).

A white sand path leads to the top of the hill where one confronts a long, blank wall; behind is the infinite expanse of blue sea. A path to the sacred — ocean, sky, white sand, retaining wall, oval lotus pond. One descends a stair straight down to the center of the pond and enters the main hall. The sun in the west shines into this room of vermilion walls and suffuses it in a reddish glow. Shadows from the pillars slant across the floor. Standing in these contrasts of light and shadow, one experiences a realm that is beyond the everyday and can turn to reflect on one's own truth". (T. Ando)

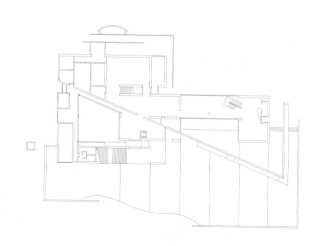

MUSEUM, NARIWA, 1991—94.

"Nariwacho, a provincial town in Okayama Prefecture, is located to the north of the city of Kurashiki. For many years it's been blessed economically because of the copper mines in the area. It's also well known for folk-houses called FUKIYA that are coloured a distinctive red ocher.

The museum is located between the site of an old residence surrounded by a stone wall and a steep slope to the south. I created another wall layer and put a concrete box in it. Visitors approaching the museum first encounter the old stone wall, that has witnessed the passage of time, and then ascend an angled ramp around the concrete box and get a visual tour of the west-facing planted slope, where a large surface of water is situated between the slope and the museum. I wanted to make the museum a place where nature, culture and history come together". (T. Ando)

CLAUDIO SILVESTRIN

"Claudio Silvestrin's integrity, clarity of mind, inventiveness and concern for details are reflected in his rigorous minimal style; austere but not extreme, contemporary yet timeless, calming but not ascetic, strong but not intimidating, elegant but not ostentatious": this is how the architect prefers to define his work.

Massimo Vignelli has also underlined these aspects, adding that: "Thanks to a lyrical sense that reminds me of Montale, and a serenity that is reminiscent of Piero della Francesca and the strength of medieval architecture, the essence of Silvestrin's work is Mediterranean, noble and peasant, intellectual and sensitive, solar and silent". [102]

Here again are a series of apparent antinomies that denote an architecture that, with patience, constancy and no lapses, has confidently embarked on the path towards a difficult, but not impossible, attempt at reconciliation.

The search for equilibrium is the central theme of Silvestrin's work, coupled with others including abstraction, the void, a sense of ground and space, the value of light and silence.

"I always try to find a balance. A balance where, for example, there is no more friction between materials or between vertical and horizontal elements. A balance where there is no contrast. The final objective is always to find a balance between lightness and weight, between voids and solids. To find a balance that is abstract but not too much, natural but not organic, to find balance and harmony".

The reconciliation and balance sought by Silvestrin go beyond purely formal aspects and involve broader themes. Mindful of AG Fronzoni's teaching, Silvestrin does not make any breaks in history, time and space. Cistercian architecture, Piet Mondrian and Lucio Fontana can all be reconciled in a project that shows the necessary open-mindeness, unburdened by intellectualisms, a project that reveals the basic shared features. Pure, immediate, unconditioned perception is the only gauge for observing the world and the only expressive possibility that surpasses the confines of codified, and therefore coercive languages incapable of seeing what is evident but obscured or misled by the corrupted historicist claims of intellectualism.

Even the space is unique and intact, seamlessly joining interior and exterior: "What matters is the act of preserving space".

While the otherwise admired Mies van der Rohe continues to dialogue with history through decisively contemporary forms and means (for example, the classical reference of the pedestal in the Barcelona Pavilion) and with external space, through the use of innovative, large glass walls, in Silvestrin's work these aspects of a self-affirmative modernity are diluted by timeless essentiality.

"The resistance of materials freezes the fashions of time", "Time suspended in stillness" and "Timeless and unsigned", are just some of Silvestrin's aphorisms that most clearly illustrate his programme for "a site configuration in which all forms of conflict cease, the eye is calmed, the cogito gives up doubting, the direction becomes clear".

"The modern architects I admire most – Van der Rohe, Barragan, Ando, Kahn and Van der Laan – have all paid attention to some of the ancient principles which may cautiously be called classical. What they have understood is the importance of interpreting classical principles without being nostalgic and without copying antique shapes and forms". Classical principles are understood by Silvestrin not just in formal terms, but rather as a way of being: a way of being that is not conditioned by contingent circumstances and contemporary noise; a way of being that takes place in timeless surroundings in which everyday actions finally acquire meaning and dignity.

To sum up, Claudio Silvestrin's minimalism can be traced back to the attempt to create scenarios for human life in which, having eliminated noise, superfluousness and anything that hinders a complete perception, we find classic serenity in the sense of the basic eternal value.

While artistic American minimalism has contributed little to Claudio Silvestrin's architecture, the influence of Cistercian architecture or a certain type of "architettura povera"

has been much more important and far-reaching. In the villa on Majorca and the house in Provence an almost mystical sense of space is combined with elements like the long stone benches inspired by local "poor" architecture, among other things, and which represent a symbol of having finally achieved a sense of being.

A sense of being that the monastic complexes affirmed through their simple, yet solid architecture that appeared to emerge from the ground and which the monks experienced by confining themselves to the place and to the choir stalls where they spent hour after hour in silence, interrupted only by chants praising God and measured in chronological terms by the rays of light moving across bare walls.

A calm, serene and satisfied sense of being, drawn to the attention of our convulsed and unsatisfied world today even by the plain stone benches standing close to the entrance door in so many Mediterranean buildings.

Citing M. Heidegger: "Living is to be in peace in a place, to remain in peace and to preserve peace by taking care of those things that disclose the sense of communion between the earth and sky, between divinity and mankind". Silvestrin emphasises his separation from today's extenuated and intellectualistic debate on architecture.

Great architecture and minor examples, mysticism and pantheism, Cistercian simplicity and Mediterranean myth are reconciled in the solid, immovable bench that Silvestrin proposes in various forms, almost to symbolise the meaning of his architecture: from the Neuendorf and Bartos houses to the Barker-Mill apartment, from the great hall in the Hombroich complex to the Girombelli apartment. For Silvestrin, the true values are ageless.

In the silence enveloping his architecture, time is unmoving and is only marked by the cycle of natural light.

Solid walls, rather than the large glass walls of the Modern Movement, enclose an internal space protected from the noise and vulgarity of an external world from which it selects certain aspects through a few, small, qualifying openings (villa on Majorca, villa in Provence, Pitti Discovery Gallery in Florence), or by direct osmosis, without the filter of a fixture which is invisible (Miro Gallery in Florence, Z apartment in Venice). Here again is a reconciliation of apparent antagonisms. Even light plays a highly significant part, but is accurately measured as in the medieval convent: light and shade. Not just the hygienic light of the Modern Movement, but the light that "returns with the footsteps of the night", bringing mankind consolation and restoring a sense of belonging to the vast physical and metaphysical entities.

"The feeling of one's own being… is intensified to its full potency once the thickness of the space surrounding one's own body manifests itself. Thus the ideal construction opens up the seeing of such thickness by erecting unadorned walls to form a pure mass of air, uncluttered and unconquered, free from the arrogant presence of man's self-assertive will.

Only through this 'clearing' is space rendered visible.

Sky and earth, divinities and mortals, Apollo and Dionysius, good and bad, science and non-visible, image and word, geometry and nature, form and function, mass and void, brightness and shadow, solidity and lightness, less and more must not be seen as one versus the other". This is how Claudio Silvestrin clearly describes the purpose of an architecture that embarks on the difficult path of simplicity, overcoming those contrasts, including ideological contrasts that are the most evident symbol of our disconnected and fragmented contemporary world.

AG Fronzoni's ethical thrust has found fertile new paths in the work of his pupil, Claudio Silvestrin, himself now master.

All of Silvestrin's work comes from afar, and this has given him solid foundations, but equally, having stripped away all that is not essential, it has the capacity of revealing the absolute novelty and miracle hidden in what is evident but no longer recognisable to our eyes.

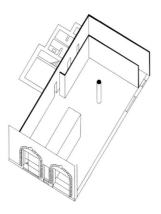

VICTORIA MIRO GALLERY, FLORENCE, 1990.

This contemporary gallery is situated on the south bank of the river Arno, known as the Lungarno Guicciardini, where it is the only façade on the tiny Piazza Scarlatti.

From Piazza Scarlatti, the gallery's façade displays two symmetrical, perfectly square single-pane 3 x 3 m windows. Incorporated into one of these windows is the entrance door, which has no dividing frame. From the inside, looking out over the Arno and Florentine architecture, the openings are unhampered by distracting window frames.

Uninterrupted expanses of white emulsioned plasterboard walls and smooth concrete floor enclose the space.

The neutral and elegant spatial layout gives full potency to the works of art.

NEUENDORF HOUSE, MAJORCA, 1989.
This structure has grown out of the land on which it stands: the rendering is made from local earth-coloured pigments mixed with lime; local Santanyi stone paves the floors, inside and out, and forms solid, immovable tables, benches and basins.

A straight, stepped path, 110 metres long, leads to the house.

The 9-metre-high outer façade is a blank, plastered wall, severed by a vertical gap. This is the threshold, the entrance leading into the empty square courtyard (12 x 12 m) which vividly frames the sky. The exterior dynamic brightness of the courtyard is a constant visual contrast to the interior stillness. From the courtyard, a large square opening leads to the pool. The 38-metre long pool forms a spectacular, shimmering projection towards the horizon. Under the pool, the construction houses a garage and a small apartment.

Everywhere here nature and architecture are contrived to interact and enhance one another.

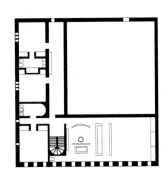

BOUTIQUE JOHAN, GRAZ, 1992.
The boutique is located on the ground floor of a sixteenth-century building and comprises two long, narrow spaces with vaulted ceilings. Although it is as modern as a shuttle, the place gives the impression of having being excavated, bringing light into a timeless cave that has been perfectly preserved, including its intact monoliths.
The lighting does justice to this serene space, providing a general sensation of light that spreads moderately throughout.
This boutique set the trend for many of the fashion stores that followed in the Nineties.

MAISON B., PROVENCE, 1992.
The conversion of an old farmhouse in the countryside between Nice and Aix-en-Provence prompted Silvestrin to create one of his works that most effectively reconciles serenity and monumentality, an innovative sense of empty space and diffused spirituality.
The predominant material is Burgundy Beauval stone, from which most of the furniture and fittings have been made, as well as the floors throughout the house. A 12-metre-long bench stretches the length of the main living room. Concealed by a massive new wall is the grand, yet simple stone staircase. This ascending and descending 'corridor' spans the full length and height of the house. It leads to all areas: first up to the guest wing, then down to the living room and then up again to the master suite of rooms: a narrow stone path forming the central axis of the house. In the master bathroom everything is sculpted from Beauval stone; two wash basins are carved into the wall-to-wall stepped counter, the curved shower screen stands like a monolith and the rounded contours of the oval bathtub reveal all the stone's sensual and enduring qualities.

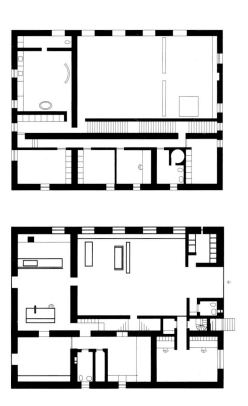

WHITE CUBE GALLERY, LONDON, 1993.
This tiny 20m² gallery is situated on the first floor of a building close to Piccadilly. By forming a geometric space within a traditional room and by screening the existing windows with diffused light, this intervention creates the illusion of being inside a cube detached from the mundane world.

BARKER-MILL APARTMENT, LONDON, 1993.
This is a conversion of an apartment inside the glass and concrete complex designed by Sir Norman Foster on the south bank of the Thames. Large slabs of serena stone from Tuscany cover the floors and a large curved satin glass screen separates the doorless kitchen and bedroom areas from the living room and study areas. The geometrical forms of the furniture throughout the apartment are all one-off designs, as are all fixtures and fittings. Numerous sophisticated details veil the technology, giving the apartment a feeling of silence and abstraction.

INSTALLATION FOR EXHIBITION BY ANISH KAPOOR, HAYWARD GALLERY, LONDON, 1998.
From time to time the Hayward Gallery of London has commissioned Silvestrin to design installations for the following exhibitions: Gravity and Grace (1993), Robert Mapplethorpe (1997), Beyond Reason (1997), Miyajima (1997), Anish Kapoor (1998), Lucio Fontana (1999). What characterises all of them is the sense of inventive perceptual transformation, as if the existing concrete edifice were to vanish as one enters the gallery.

Installation for exhibition by Lucio Fontana, Hayward Gallery, London, 1999.
A long bench for contemplating the works of one of the favourite masters.

GIROMBELLI APARTMENT, MILANO, 1999.
A 14-metre-long satin glass wall separates the day and night zones. Sunlight travels uninterrupted, both from east and west, through this wall that divides and unites. The floor is made from white stone slabs, as are the benches and one-off bathroom fixtures.
The fact of not commissioning the architect to complete the furnishings was detrimental, in part, to the overall completion of the work.

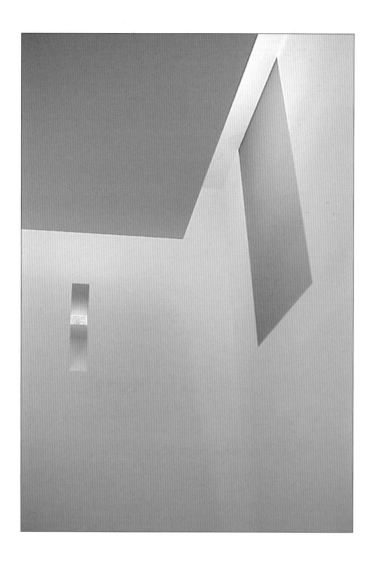

PITTI DISCOVERY GALLERY, FLORENCE, 1999.
Large stone slabs and white plaster create a small gallery measuring just 23 square metres. The two large, existing windows were partially reduced. The light is diffused from a high source and a small transparent window allows a glimpse of the sky and part of a tree.
This space is also dominated by a strong feeling of inwardness.

GIORGIO ARMANI STORE, PARIS, 1999.
Located in the beautiful Place Vendôme, this space stands out for its diffuse use of the same stone as in the square. The stone from Place Vendôme invades the interior floors and walls, creating a timeless atmosphere.
A basin of water at the entrance reconnects the modern store with the vaster dimensions that overcome contingencies and immediate functional requirements. An absolute novelty are the light fittings made from metal plate which conceal the light sources so that a mysterious luminous aura is diffused onto the walls.

CAFFÉ ILLY, TRIESTE, 2000.
The new image created by Claudio Silvestrin for Caffé Illy has been developed to give a feeling of comfort and serenity. The visual order of the elegant and simple design lines and natural materials induce the eyes and mind to relax, to salvage the "lusso della pausa", far from the bustle of our daily lives. The use of timber and natural stone helps to create a warm, welcoming interior. A contemporary yet timeless space.
-natural materials: stone for the floor and the lower part of the walls, marmorino with the same colour for the upper part, zebra wood for the furniture, coffee-coloured oxidised brass for the counter and the internal tables.
-earth/water binomial: stone, marmorino and wood referring to the colours of the land. Fragments of blue light and the basin referring to water element.
-space: low stone walls divide the space into zones.
-visual orientation: clear direction made by the stretched elements like the counter, the wooden bench and the low wall.
-services: concealed.
-counter: a brass monolithic object with cut-outs for sugar, napkins, ashtray, and waste.
-walls: a continuous, curved line around the space with carved niches to house the merchandise and very small niches to house single coffee cups. A long niche for glasses and bottles behind the bar counter.
-window: a big screen of sand blasted glass cut with a stripe of clear glass emphasises the feeling of privacy and intimacy. Inner space and outer space are beckoning each other. The cut is to intensify the illy cup/symbol, which appears to be suspended from gravity.

GIORGIO ARMANI SHOP, MILAN, 2000.
Following his commission to design the Giorgio Armani boutique in Place Vendôme in Paris which opened at the end of last year, Claudio Silvestrin has been asked to design all of the Giorgio Armani boutiques worldwide. It is the first time that Armani has allowed an architect to put his name to one of his stores. The second store in the project to be completed is the Giorgio Armani boutique in Milan's via Sant Andrea.
The enormous 1000-square metre flagship store in the heart of Milan's fashion district continues the theme developed for Place Vendôme. Silvestrin describes it as a style that transcends minimalism and instead strives for timeless elegance. One of the distinguishing features of the store is a dramatic 50-metre long perspective view of the double-height space seen from outside the store through the window, or from the top of the stairs inside. The walls and floor are raw French limestone and the furniture, designed by Silvestrin, is Macassar ebony.

CANAL BUILDING APARTMENT, LONDON, 2001.

This 120-square metre loft/apartment faces Regent's Canal in Islington. It was originally a 100-square metre concrete shell with two large terraces placed on the roof of a 1920's warehouse.

The intervention preserves the uninterrupted north-south views and maximises natural light.

Through a 5-metre tall door we enter the living space to face one floating base white wall which is opposite a 12-metre stretch of wall cupboards which conceal the functions of daily life, from laundry to books.

Behind the bare wall is hidden a children's bedroom, a generous wetroom and stairs leading to the mezzanine where a study desk and a sleeping area are located.

This monolithic space is furnished and built with the minimum number of elements, furniture and natural materials: Lecce stone for the floor, the basins and the kitchen island unit; the pear wood of the dining table and the staircase; the matt white paint for cupboards, wall and the vaulted ceiling. The sofa, table, basins and lighting are Claudio Silvestrin prototypes now produced by several manufacturers.

Donnelly Gallery, Ireland, 1999–2001.
Marie Donnelly: "Claudio Silvestrin's work is pure. The simple use of natural materials binds the spaces he has created, or designed, to the external landscape. Claudio is inflexible in his pursuit of pure form. This calls for a certain degree of trust on the client's behalf. Living in one of his interiors is an act of will. When we first contacted Claudio and asked him to design a building, after he had visited the site, I asked him for an immediate answer. He took a blank sheet of paper and drew two parallel lines at the top of the page."
The building, which is both house and gallery, overlooks the Irish Sea. The rich vegetation partially conceals the new construction which stretches longitudinally for 89 metres. The roof and floor are, graphically speaking, two horizontal lines mirroring the sea horizon and piercing through the trees like shooting lines directed towards infinity and, at the same time, sandwiching the living space.

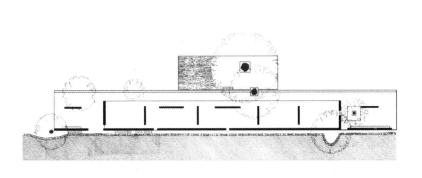

JOHN PAWSON

The partnership between John Pawson and Claudio Silvestrin ended, after three years of collaboration and a unity of intents that had enabled them to emerge in the international panorama as the absolute protagonists of minimalist architecture, at the moment of choosing the colour for the villa on Majorca.

According to Silvestrin, the villa was to be the same colour, in fact made from the same material, as the earth around it, whereas in Pawson's opinion it should have been white.

The different training of the two architects came to the fore on this occasion, together with the differences that, subsequently, distinguished their respective careers. The radical manner in which this apparently secondary question was tackled provides a clear testimony to the diversity and the subtle, but major differences that connote and enliven the panorama of minimalist architecture.

The "noble and peasant, intellectual and sensitive" Claudio Silvestrin (M. Vignelli), in a gesture of absolute simplicity, inevitably preferred a mixture made from the surrounding soil, whereas the colder John Pawson was bound to choose a colour like white, immune from any reference to the Mediterranean nature of the building, in order to affirm the necessary distance from anything that might even restrict the work to a precise location.

Compared to Silvestrin, who focuses more on the search for equilibrium, Pawson's work, in toto, appears to denote a greater request for abstraction. Even the notion of suspended time, one that is difficult to recognise, in which the works of both architects are set, is expressed differently: time that wears away and corrodes in Silvestrin, and an unchanging, almost frozen time in Pawson.

The four years he spent teaching at Nagoya University in Japan in the mid Seventies undoubtedly contributed to shaping his work and, as Bruce Chatwin writes, underlining the pertinent value of the Japanese notion of 'wabi': "He trained his eye on Japanese buildings, from the most venerated temples to the simplest peasant house. To this friendship with the architect, Shiro Kuramata, he owes the insight that you can make the most daring experiments with new materials and new technology without having to sacrifice the spirit of poverty". [103]

The time spent in Japan, together with the widespread and extensive cultural and spiritual rediscoveries of Zen philosophy, substantiated a concept of architectural "poverty" which Pawson linked to Western proposals put forward by Mies van der Rohe, the Shakers and Cistercian architecture to develop a particular conception of space, empty and free from visual and abstract encumbrances.

"What is generally recognized is that 'emptiness' in architecture – or empty space – is not empty, but full; yet to realise this fullness requires the most exacting standards and discipline from the architect. Here, there can be no room for uncertainty, or anxious 'artistic' effects. Either the work must be perfect, or not at all.

Architecture is 'frozen music': the more you reduce, the more perfect its notes must be". [104]

Pawson's formal reduction stands out for this final freezing, which gives an idea of the incorruptibility of its interiors.

According to Deyan Sudjic: "For Pawson, architectural reduction is a process that takes you through a mirror. You pass through the point at which a room is merely empty, and emerge out on the other side, in that mirror world to discover richness in the subtle differences between five shades of white, and the sense of release that comes from allowing a wall to flow in space unencumbered by visual distractions". And, again, "In one sense Pawson's architecture is an exercise in control, in lifting the sense of oppression that comes from the clutter of things, and the visual chaos of superfluous complexity. It seeks to eliminate the distraction of awkward proportions and the constant irritation of the catch that does not function unobtrusively. In its place he offers the comfort of exactness, of small things done well". [105]

Phrases like these, albeit extremely pertinent, perhaps fail to capture that sense of distance, translated into an exasperated search for abstraction, that Pawson aimed to place between everyday rituals and their sublimation.

Many of Pawson's settings appear to be aimed at a sort of spiritual type elevation, a combination of Zen philosophy and the Calvinistic spirit: these include the bathroom in the Van Royen apartment (1986), the austere living room in the Rothman apartment (1990), in which the bath is also resolved using a parallelepiped of Carrara marble, the filters linking the exterior in the form of the satin-finish glazing at the Wakaba restaurant (1987) and the Cannelle shop (1988), as well as the almost sacred feel of the geometric courtyard in the Pawson House (1995).

The unease induced by our convulsive modern and contemporary world, according to W. Worringer, and also according to the Modern Movement which adopted the peculiarly impractical white as the symbolic colour of the new architecture, can only be suspended by an accentuation of abstraction, understood as "a point of tranquillity and a refuge from appearances". [106]

"These regular abstract forms are ... the only ones and the highest, in which man can rest in the face of the vast confusion of the world-picture". [107]

Michael Speaks' comments really seems to find their mark when he warns that: "Perhaps a more accurate comparison of Pawson's design process might be made with the Shakers, or 'Shaking Quakers', as their English founders were called before departing from Manchester for America.

Indeed, even Chatwin's own experience of the Pawson interior he visited in London is more reminiscent of the Shaking Quaker than it is of the devotee of wabi: "I walked around the walls, watching its planes, shadows, and proportions in a state of near-elation. Shakers, like the devotees of wabi, took an oath of worldly poverty, abstaining from sex and from general commerce with the external world. Moreover, they were forbidden to make or use ornamental or stylized products of any description.

(...) Shaker interiors reduce unwanted ornamental features in order to intensify, rather than reduce, the sensual experience of the divine.

Like the Shakers, Pawson subtracts unwanted materials – he calls them clutter – in order to isolate and recombine those selected materials into his own architectural idiom". [108]

Also for W. Worringer, a pioneering theoretician of a relationship between a state of unease induced by the external world and the need for abstraction, one possible way out might be to take the individual thing "out of its arbitrariness and seeming fortuitousness, of eternalising it by approximation to abstract forms and, in this manner, of finding a point of tranquillity and a refuge from appearances". [109]

Every process exploring function and every solution or detail consequently elaborated by Pawson obeys this unsuppressed requirement.

An exclusive use of the straight line, its combination using orthogonality and a decisive abstraction of functions (the Obumex kitchen, stereometric baths, wooden furniture that clearly identifies and protects the living areas, as in Tilty Hill barn, in the waiting areas for Cathay Pacific and in the Faggionato apartment), lead to that state of tranquillity pursued by his architecture in general through an exemplary simplicity of design.

"What I look for is the excitement of empty space. It has the capacity to bring architecture alive, just as it does a Chinese scroll painting. Emptiness allows us to see space as it is, to see architecture as it is, preventing it from being corrupted, or hidden, by the incidental debris of paraphernalia of everyday life. It offers the space, both psychological and physical, for contemplation, and the serenity that can encourage meditative quiet and calm, without the jarring distraction of possessions". [110]

Pawson's attempt comes closer to the intransigent ascetic spirit of the severely puritanical Dutch Calvinist churches, made even more famous by Pieter Saerendam's paintings, rather than to a Mediterranean pantheism in the classical sense.

His strong propensity to abstraction, the millimetric and perennial search for aristocratic formal perfection, the use of noble materials like marble or fine woods, the cold authoritativeness of his interiors that aspire to expressive solutions with a touch of mastery and finality, the predilection for colours like white or grey, decline John Pawson's architecture of simplicity in a sense that is steeped in asceticism reminiscent, in all probability, of strict protestant ethics.

The paths leading to minimalism may be conceived in the most widely varied geographical and cultural settings and, as in Pawson's case, use a convergence of previously irreconcilable ideological elements, Zen philosophy and Shaker puritanism, in the name of a syncretism whose goal is the affirmation of a common need for simplicity.

VICTORIA MIRO HOUSE, LONDON, 1988.
Pawson included a series of formal solutions in the refurbishment of a Victorian house in Hampstead which he used in many of his later projects: large strips of Japanese oak in the floors, white walls interposed by essential cupboards, acid-etched glass that uniformly diffuses the external light. Stone is used in the main bathroom and a circular marble basin serves as the wash basin. The oak staircase, visually detached from the walls, loses gravity and rises towards the light.

ROTHMAN APARTMENT, LONDON, 1990.
A deep row of central cupboards divides the living area from the sleeping area without losing the feeling of a single space. The kitchen is divided off by a simple low wall. The two doorless bedrooms lead into the bathroom with a stepped floor and bath tub in Carrara marble. All the furnishings and furniture are one-off items. Every aspect is carefully designed to give a sense of calm, emphasised by the diffused light and the exacting use of natural materials. The living room contains a long bench and single metaphysical armchair highlighted by a light source overhead.

Van Royen Apartment, London, 1991.
Pawson creates a residence-cum-gallery for an art dealer from the conversion of a Victorian apartment. The exhibition spaces, office and library take up most of the apartment, whereas the smaller rooms are reserved for private life. These include the geometrical and essential kitchen containing a wooden table and high cupboards that conceal all the usual kitchen accessories.

Pawson House, London, 1995.
The interiors of this Victorian building were completely gutted and redesigned to create one of the most famous works of Minimal London.
On the mezzanine floor, a room with two fireplaces and a long stone bench, which is used for seating, as a focal point and a source of light. The wooden table is unconnected in the longitudinal sense, creating a vanishing point that runs parallel to the vanishing point of the long, uncut floorboards in Douglas pine.
Benches, specially designed wooden stools and just two chairs furnish one of the most photographed rooms in the house.
The light wooden staircase between two walls reflects the models used earlier, as does the geometrical bath tub standing in the centre of the bathroom to underline the exceptional nature of the most humble elements and the most ordinary functions.

CALVIN KLEIN STORE, NEW YORK, 1995.
Stone floors, white walls and meticulous precision
for the store at the corner of Madison Avenue
belonging to an equally essential designer.

TILTY BARN, TILTY HILL, ESSEX, 1996.
In this conversion and reuse of an old barn, Pawson introduces a few, terse elements that allow a new residential use. The structures are conserved, but with the addition of a new poured concrete floor, low walls and generous unframed windows. There is a seamless relationship with the exterior. The large living room with the fireplace creates a particularly dramatic effect, in which a few low walls define the living area underlined by the special sofa element with its high, enveloping wooden structure.

JIGSAW STORE, LONDON, 1996.
Pawson was commissioned to design the flagship store for what was soon to become an internationally well-known brand, destined to be copied repeatedly by the vulgate minimalism.
By removing all the partitions and part of the floor from the first storey, Pawson creates two retail spaces that lead, down a monumental staircase illuminated along the edge of the side wall, to the lower level of the offices.
The effect from the street is one of striking simplicity and, at the same time, monumentality created by the two large crosses of the window mullions. Inside the store, the stone floors, white walls, stereometric furniture and etched glass screens explore the possibilities of this empty space with sophisticated simplicity.

CATHAY PACIFIC WAITING AREA, HONG-KONG AIRPORT, 1998.

Inside the airport designed by Sir Norman Foster at Chek Lap Kok, Pawson was commissioned to create the passenger lounges for the national airline.

Within Foster's high-tech structure, Pawson inserts the solid simplicity, not only in formal terms, of a series of furnishings (floors and stairs in hammered granite and wooden furniture) which make his work, in fact of secondary importance, look like the romanesque pedestal for the gothic cathedral above.

Order, natural materials and etched glass, which filter a light that almost seems natural, act as a buffer against the noise and stress caused by the flight and the chaos of an airport designed for an annual capacity of 35 million passengers, a figure that has already been exceeded.

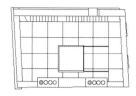

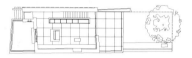

PAWSON HOUSE, LONDON, 1999.

Pawson created a second house for his own use through the refurbishment of a typical London residential building. The exterior façade was left intact, but the interiors have been completely redesigned. From the entrance, where you glimpse the staircase leading down to the dining area and the garden, you walk into the living room with a fireplace, a long stone bench and a sofa with a special wooden surface that also doubles as a desk. In the dining area below, part of the Obumex kitchen system, designed by Pawson in 1996, seems to continue into the garden. The ground floor leads up to the master bedroom with adjoining bathroom. Above, are the two children's rooms, divided by the bathroom, facing onto the stairwell where a long desk has been installed for work and study.

Millimetric formal and functional precision are coupled with genuine inventions: the long, stone bath tub in the master bathroom doubles as both bath and wash basin, whereas the roof of the second bathroom can be opened, weather permitting, to allow the experience of bathing outdoors.

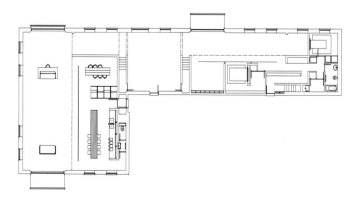

Faggionato Apartment, London, 1999.
The conversion of the Piper building to residential use forms part of a general London programme for the reutilisation of disused industrial-type buildings in the Fulham area. The building was named after the decorative balconies added by John Piper during a preliminary conversion phase of the building belonging to the Gas Board.
Pawson has used the L-shaped building to create, on the ground floor, the living room, kitchen and service premises, with the bedrooms and study on the first floor mezzanines.
Oak floors, white walls, lights along the tops of the walls and etched glass give the setting a sense of calm and consummate tranquillity.

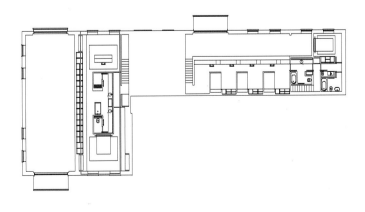

PETER ZUMTHOR

His training as a cabinet-maker, before studying design at the Kunstgewerbeschule in Basel and architecture at the Pratt Institute in New York, certainly marked not only the beginnings but most of Zumthor's relatively late professional activities. The architect can now boast a few outstanding works, most of which are located within the close geographical confines of the upper Rhine valley between Chur and the Saint Gothard pass, in the Swiss canton of Graubünden.

Apart from the group of residential buildings at Biel-Benken outside Basel (1989–96) and the Kunsthaus in Bregenz (1990–97), this isolated district contains all Zumthor's works: the enclosure for a Roman archaeological site (Chur, 1985–86), the architect's own studio (Haldenstein, 1985–86), the Sogn Benedetg chapel (Sumvitg, 1985–88), a housing project for the elderly (Chur, 1989–93), Gugalun house (Versam, 1990–94) and the thermal bath at Vals (1990–96) which, together with the Arts Centre in Bregenz, has attracted the attention of architectural critics and brought international acclaim to his work.

The value of the construction materials is exceptionally important in all these buildings: wood, reinforced concrete, stone, glass. Materials which form a skin, or veneer over the solid structures, giving the architecture a surprising sense of extreme lightness.

In the enclosure for the archaeological site at Chur, the wooden structure rises up from a solid reinforced concrete base and is clad with wooden panels that allow air and light to circulate inside. Traditionally local shapes and materials are given abstract form and enclose the few antique remains without any compromising effect or any desire for eloquence.

Other examples of supreme craftsmanship can be found in the external cladding of the Zumthor studio, an ample but simple volume flanked by the rectilinear stair block which seems to resume, and also refine, the vertical theme of the wooden palings around the nearby vegetable gardens, and the chapel of Sogn Benedetg where the traditional wooden roof planks are also used for the vertical walls. Time ("Like the old farmhouses – the wood – will darken in the sunlight and become black on the south side and silver-gray on the northern one.") will correct and blend this architecture even more completely with the landscape.

The chapel interior is made entirely from wood: including the most delicate structures, the floor – which is separated from the walls to give a sensation of floating – the roof and the simple, straight pews which give order and direction to the unusual curved and enveloping ground plan.

Even in the severe residential complex for the elderly in Chur, the tufa cladding and fine detailing of the windows and wooden structures soften the rigorous planivolumetric layout, giving a sense of almost oriental lightness.

A degree of sophisticated but at the same time meditated attention to local building styles emerges in the Gugalun house, the extension of a small, isolated, traditional rural building.

The traditional wooden elements are given abstract form by introducing horizontal bands to clad a partition alternatively placed horizontally and vertically, reminiscent of hollowed tree trunks. Using an operation of subtraction, Zumthor replaces the trunks of the existing building with a light partition, thus giving depth and thickness to the new external walls in a skillful compositional device. The simple, elemental modularity of the existing building is reproposed, without mimicry, and enhanced with technical and formal devices to give it unusual new possibilities. Antique techniques and materials again play a significant role in the context of design that is sensitive to the environment, tradition, time and the changes to materials wrought by the latter.

The finely woven stone skin of the thermal bath in Vals undergoes an ulterior, extreme decantation process leading to the external cladding in even and uniform glass panels, simply attached to a thin metal structure, at the Kunsthaus in Bregenz.

In Vals and in Bregenz, Zumthor uses cladding once again: the reinforced concrete structure of the baths and a composite structure in concrete and iron for the Kunsthaus. The ascetic, but not as aseptic rigour of his two greatest works is softened by the modulations of the surfaces which are extremely sensitive to the intensity of light.

In Vals, the use of rough stone and extreme spatial simplicity give the water-filled settings a sort of archaic and primordial connotation: "So our bath is not a showcase for the latest aquagadgetry, water jets, nozzles or chutes. It relies instead on the silent, primary experiences of bathing, cleansing oneself, and relaxing in the water; on the body's contact with water at different temperatures and in different kinds of spaces; on touching stone".

The monolithic stone mass of the bath in Vals seems to have been excavated rather than built to house the necessary functions. Its monumental interiors are filled with silence and an antique sense of calm and peace, lacking any evident contemporary connotations.

In Bregenz, the stereometric Kunsthaus building is particularly sensitive to the intensity of light reflected by the lake, which it overlooks, and the vast, changing sky. At night, it looks like a friendly lamp.

"From the outside, the building looks a lamp. It absorbs the changing light of the sky, the haze of the lake, it reflects light and color and gives an intimation of its inner life according to the angle of vision, the daylight and the weather".

The stunning effect of dematerialising a building that is in fact built in reinforced concrete and metal is achieved with extraordinary simplicity: an external cladding in simple glass panels. "The outer skin of the building consists of finely etched glass, it looks like slightly ruffled feathers or like a scaly structure of large glass panels. The glass panels, which are all the same size, are neither perforated nor cut. They rest on metal consoles, held in place by large clamps. The edges of the glass are exposed. The wind wafts through the open joints of the scaly structure. Lake air penetrates the fine mesh of the space-framework, of the steel structure of the self-bearing facade, which rises from the pit of the basement and embraces, without firm contact, the interior of the monolithic spatial sculpture with a differentiated system of facade glazing, heat insulation and shading... Reduced to static essentials... the construction, material and visual form of the building constitute a unified whole. The building is exactly what we see and touch, exactly what we feel beneath our feet: a cast concrete, stony body".

In this sense, owing to his capacity to allow things to be perceived for what they really are, Zumthor should be regarded as one of the most radically minimalist architects.

His successful attempt to give concrete form, using space, volumes and surfaces, to the abstract requirements of a contemporary idea of simplicity is ultimately based on a sense of place, rather than on an aesthetic formula.

Quoting Martin Heidegger, Zumthor repeats that the philosopher gave the title "'Bauen, Wohnnen, Denken' to an essay with his reflections on what it means when men build homes and live in specific places. Building, dwelling, and thinking are activities which belong together and which men use as ways to learn about and be part of the world. Heidegger observed that our thinking, as abstract as it may seem, is closely connected with our experience of place. This has something to do with the fact that man exists in places, that it is from places that he forms his relationships with the world – or simply, that he lives in the world". [111]

SOGN BENEDETG CHAPEL, SUMVITG, CANTON OF GRAUBÜNDEN, 1985–88.
The chapel is built from the same material as the old farmhouses in the area. Over time, the wood will harden and acquire the natural nuances that will enable the small building to blend even more completely with the landscape and its history. The unusual leaf-shaped ground plan, with a single central hall, intends to emphasise the chapel's dedication to the Virgin Mary by recalling maternal forms.
The extreme simplicity of the perimetric cladding resumes the typical local roofing method. The chapel interior is remarkable for a sort of floating floor, a radius of simple uprights, the geometrical order of the pews and zenithal lighting.

STUDIO ZUMTHOR, HALDENSTEIN, CANTON OF GRAUBÜNDEN, 1985–86.
Masterly use of wood, reminiscent of the architect's initial training as a cabinet-maker, and subtle linguistic updates are combined to create a work that does not intend to stand out from its surroundings right away, but on the contrary is reserved for a more careful, in-depth perusal, revealing a myriad of exciting surprises. A selected use of materials, attention to detail, a sense of participation in the natural surroundings, a simple spatial layout, and an up-to-date but not overemphatic linguistic vocabulary of artistic derivation make this work an "object" that is easily reconciled with the environment, but at the same time constantly points to new ways of achieving constructive simplicity.

GUGALUN HOUSE, VERSAM, CANTON OF GRAUBÜNDEN, 1990–94.
In this extension of a small wooden farm building, which is at least two hundred years old, Zumthor further develops the technique of using pre-existing structures as a means of achieving innovation through continuity.
The trunks of the old construction are replaced by planks positioned to give the same idea of thickness, almost as if using hollowed trunks. The cladding for the new construction consists of wooden planks arranged alternatively vertically and horizontally. A new geometry flanks the old.
The sense of continuity that is the dominant feature of the work enhances the ageless value of the natural materials and their geometric pattern gives substance to and updates the timeless construction methods.

Thermal Bath, Vals, Canton of Graubünden, 1990–96.

"You enter… through an odd bronze turnstile. On one side is a fairly dark concrete wall; spring water flows out of bronze pipes in five regularly spaced square alcoves, splashing the walls and escaping through a channel. On the other side is a stone wall with five doors; the frames are made of lacquered red mahogany and the door itself is a thick piece of black leather. They lead to changing rooms, also lined with red, lacquered wood.

A long balcony and a ramp lead down to a series of starkly geometric rooms. The concrete ceiling, pierced with thin strips of light, weighs heavily over a grotto-like room with angular walls. Small yellow lights hanging from wires seem more like lightning bugs than real lamps. Everything, including the walls, floors, benches and enormous pillars, is made of the same greenish-grey gneiss with a shimmer of mica.

Several swimming pools are scattered throughout this cavern, along with a larger outdoor pool.

The water is luminous.

Various paths lead through the rugged cavities, with narrow aquatic corridors. The room housing the 'hot' pool is painted Pompeii red; arnica flower petals are floating on the surface of another pool. A monumental gilt and glass doorway leads to the terraces outside.

The valley fog mingles with the steam from the baths. In early summer, farmers graze their animals near the baths… and in winter everything is blanketed under snow.

It has been many years since a building has expressed such an eternal sense of peace with so much harmony". (François Chaslin)

Kunsthaus, Bregenz, 1990–97.
"The outer skin of the building consists of finely etched glass. It looks like slightly ruffled feathers or like a scaly structure of large glass panels.
The glass panels, which are all the same size, are neither perforated nor cut. They rest on metal consoles, held in place by large clamps. The edges of the glass are exposed.
The multi-layered facade is an autonomous wall construction that harmonizes with the interior and acts as a weather skin, daylight modulator, sun shade, and thermal insulator.
The ceilings of the exhibition rooms… consist of light trapped in glass.
Open-jointed glass panels with exposed edges hang individually from the concrete ceiling on hundreds of thin steel rods.
A sea of glass panels.
We feel how the building absorbs the daylight, the position of the sun… and we are aware of the modulation of light caused by the invisible and yet perceptible outside environment". (Peter Zumthor)

162

EDUARDO SOUTO DE MOURA

The same accusation of repetitive monotony levied by the critics against Tadao Ando's work could also apply to Souto de Moura who, for the last twenty years or more, has dedicated himself, almost exclusively, to designing single-family residences whose differences can be perceived and appraised only through a careful observation of the details, the use of materials or slight differences in plan.

Rightly, the two architects have not resented this interpretation, aware that the richness of their own work consists in the reproposal, over time, of a few, fundamental requests, verified on each occasion in relation to the geographic location, the surroundings and the client's requests.

"I began my profession as an architect designing houses and today, although not as much as before, I still like to design them.

In the History of Architecture, there is probably no more complex and difficult tipology than that of the 'house'. To design a house is the equivalent – close to paranoia – of reducing the world to a vital object.

Since 1977 I have designed dozens of houses with different briefs and contexts: urban houses, rural houses, small houses for a single person, houses for families, houses in the south, houses in the mountains, vacation houses, permanent houses, houses of one floor, houses on various floors with a lift.

Here… I admit that, in spite of the diversity of places and briefs, there is a permanent obsession with a building 'type', a kind of design persecution.

The constructive system is always the same: walls, ceilings and pavements as planes, built out of reinforced concrete and when necessary a steel column out of the context (to help with the meaning of spaces).

The outer wall is either in plastered brick or stone, according to the local atmosphere.

The remainder of the openings between the walls are closed with glass, with aluminium or wooden frames being used according to the taste and the allocated budget.

The house typology is almost always laid out on one floor – as it integrates better – varying according to the geographical context.

In the north the houses are narrow and long, with a corridor closed to the exterior, with a perimeter wall that continues and defines the lot.

Whereas in the south the houses are usually isolated units sited at the top of a small mount with the various interior spaces laid around a central courtyard.

It was this theme of the topography that led me to break the unitary volume into fragments, for better adaptation to the site topography.

Today I still design houses … and I admit that they are – one way or another – different".

The most significant contribution of Souto de Moura's research to a continuous appraisal of the real possibilities for the idea of simplicity, under the most varied conditions, lies in the minimal difference between one building and another, between yesterday's detail and today's.

Contrary to our modern aseptic clocks, sundials marked time, also meteorological time, using a simple straight rod fixed on a plane, which had to be adapted, in terms of length and orientation, to its particular setting. Like ancient sundials, Souto de Moura's numerous, apparently identical, simple and linear houses record and enliven the passing of time and light whose physicality becomes an essential element for these residential settings.

The dominant use of natural materials possessing a 'depth' that cannot be found in modern industrial products enhances this feeling of the density of a space from which the residential settings are cut out.

"The apparent simplicity of images always forces tortuous built solutions, like the manipulation of thicknesses and materials. How can an interior wall protrude into the exterior with the same appearance and depth?

In the houses that I have been designing, everything is pre-determined: light that aligns with pieces of furniture, generous glass surfaces that bring natural light inside, long interior walls without side openings, simply top lit.

The houses that I am now designing are less 'black and white', they have variations: sometimes the volume 'decomposes' in parts, the plans are no longer with full straight angles".

The element that most strongly characterises Souto de Moura's works seen in the context of architectural simplicity is his method of proceeding by geometric fragments: the walls that run from the exterior into the interior, the rectangular swimming pools, the external paving in different materials that join to provide pathways, the autonomous glazed partitions. Through a sort of physical interpretation of the aesthetic precepts of Mondrian and the De Stijl movement, Souto de Moura emphasises an intentional and planned incompleteness of a building method whose foundations lie in the use of geometric segments.

One of the architect's earliest works was the reconversion of a small ruined building in Gerés (1980). The stark, new interventions (glazed wall facing the sea and flat roof supported by a circular pillar) communicate with the existing stone structure. The intervention is interstitial, almost subdued and not affirmative. The exuberant surrounding nature and the materials of the old building attenuate the impact of the new and remain the protagonists of a successful, old relationship.

In later works, like the Braga market (1980), S.E.C. (1981), the second house at Nevogilde (1983), the annexes of Vilarinha (1986), the house in via Boavista, Porto (1987) which reuses stones and architectural elements salvaged from a ruin, Baiao house (1990), where again the construction emerges from old ruins and uses salvaged elements, Souto de Moura consolidated this approach, finding the results more successful than research which tends to dissolve rather than integrate the architectural artefact in its natural setting.

Abstraction (from Mondrian to D. Judd) and nature find a rare equilibrium in Souto de Moura.

The geometric fragments positioned by the architect on the ground and used to construct disaggregated volumes do not aspire to strong affirmations of existence but, instead, are left aside faced with the magnificence of the natural spectacle which they help to enhance, highlighting its lights and shadows, reflections and glare, sharpness and nuances, like a sheet or the gnomonic plane.

"Today I design doors and windows. There is more to light and shadow, there is a filtered, hierarchic twilight zone".

Like the Monet of Rouen cathedrals, Souto de Moura is preparing to continue his exploration of the infinite series of differences offered by the same theme.

"Evidently, the themes are always the same, of course. Each one has only it's own theme and it's inside it that it moves". (T. Bernhard)

Municipal Market, Braga, 1980–84.
A long wall, a flat roof on two neat rows of columns: few elements of neoplasticistic derivation and a sense of ruin and incompleteness, which can also be found in much of his later work.

CASA DAS ARTES, S.E.C. CULTURAL CENTRE, PORTO, 1981–88.
Sited within an existing garden, the long building was designed to blend with the vegetation. It houses an auditorium, an exhibition space and a cinema. Outside, the simple architecture reveals straight walls in concrete and stone surmounted by a flat copper roof.

CASA 2 IN NOVOGILDE, PORTO, 1983–88.
Erected in a surplus plot, the residential building looks onto the garden and its unusual and irregular ground plan is accentuated by the unfinished appearance of the load-bearing walls and the construction of a row of pillars of varying heights that reinforce the impression of a work in progress.

VILARINHA REARRANGEMENT AND EXTERNAL BUILDINGS, PORTO, 1986–88.
The project entailed the external rearrangement of an existing house designed by José Porto for the producer Manuel de Oliveira. Souto de Moura's intervention is designed to look older than the Thirties house, through the use of simple geometric devices and existing natural elements: rock, grass, the pond turned into a pool. Strong, ageless walls appropriate and protect a sophisticated play of accurately matched or jointed surfaces.

ALCANENA HOUSE, TORRES NOVAS, 1987–92.
The three building blocks are gathered around a square, central courtyard, although no windows look onto it, and a circle is traced on the paving of the court which recalls the path leading through the surrounding vineyards.
Disguised Roman citations are diluted in the plani-volumetric breakdown of a building that loses volume and solidity after a re-interpretation of the structural and compositional elements, giving preference to low wall partitions extended well beyond the static requirements. Even the apparent centripetal vocation of the building is contradicted by numerous openings on the external facades, overlooking the countryside. The stark, metaphysical central courtyard only acts as the memory.

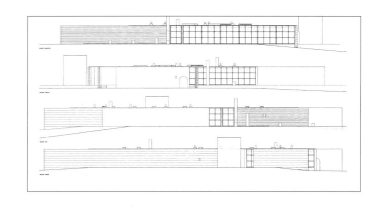

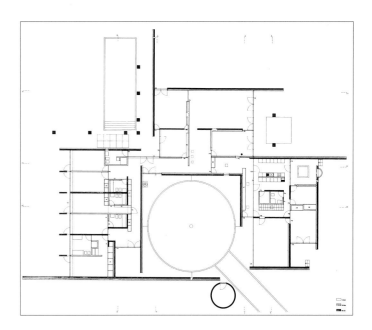

House in via Boavista, Porto, 1987–94.
"This house is a collage of others that I have made: the House of the Arts, those in Alcanena, and Vilarinha.
It was built using stones from a convent school and a ruin which was known as "The Sleeping Beauty." The stones are false, that is, they serve as a kind of mineral paint, attached to a wall which is in fact made of concrete; the source serves as a window, the balcony step and the cornises spread throughout the elevation do not comply with the stereotomy". (E. Souto de Mura)

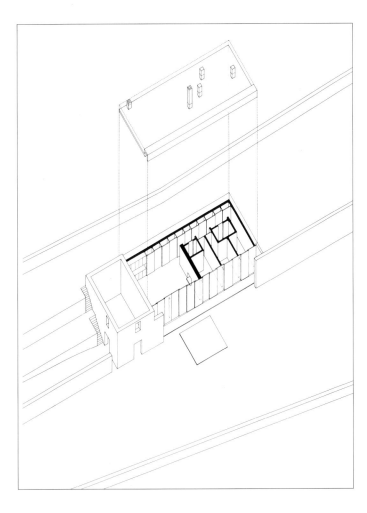

BAIAO HOUSE, BAIAO, 1990–93.
Souto de Moura uses the conversion of a small ruined building to create a holiday house that can only just be singled out in the landscape overlooking the river Douro.
The new building in reinforced concrete has an accessible, flat, grass-covered roof. Part of the existing building, alongside, has been left in its ruined state. An extensive wall with windows, whose thin mullions resemble a pergola, provides air and light for the simple interior.

MAIA HOUSE, MAIA, 1990–93.

"No excuses can be made for this house built in Maia; despite the problems that come with any project, it turned out as I intended. There was no need to justify its form, typology or system of construction. This may seem strange, but that's the way it was. It so happens that I was client and the architect" (E. Souto de Moura).

The uncertainty may persist that an increased use of fine materials (stainless steel and marble fixtures) and more finishing and protective elements (covers on external masonry partitions, for example) might have been detrimental, in part, because, having lost the "poverty" of earlier examples, the building has to a certain extent cooled the most poetic urge of the work, which was instead based on the sense of passing time. The alterations and wear on materials caused by time brings the building closer to resembling privileged nature.

RESTORATION OF MONASTERY OF SANTA MARIA DE BOURO, BRAGA, 1989.
The same level of care and attention to detail are used, wherever possible, in this complex restoration work as are experimented in the numerous residential buildings.

CONVERSION OF AN APARTMENT, PORTO, 1986–90.
Memories of the years (1974–79) spent working with Alvaro Siza come to the fore in this conversion project. The staircase without a banister and the geometric hearth introduce strong geometric elements which are softened by the curved line which the architect increasingly wishes to re-include in his linguistic repertoire, after years of being restricted to the use of rigidly orthogonal straight lines.

COMPLEX OF HOUSES WITH COURTYARD, MATOSINHOS, 1993.
Long, low, horizontal walls enclose the private grounds of a complex of residential buildings surrounding a courtyard, with flat roofs and large open areas.
The defensive character and the closure of the private areas to the outside is emphasised by the inclusion of stone walls which interact with the simple geometry of the gardens and the rectangular pools, giving the complex a feeling of openness towards nature lacking any precise connotations and is almost timeless.
The use of stone walls, like the use of ruins in earlier works, substantiates a physical perception of the matter and the natural data, avoiding any lapse in a sort of Mediterranean metaphysics, now exaggerated, that denotes so many vulgarisations by imitators.

ALBERTO CAMPO BAEZA

Having been assimilated in the lists of minimalist architecture with no initial or clear-cut refusal of the term on his behalf, Campo Baeza subsequently detached himself to some extent, preferring to describe his architecture as "essential". His name continues to feature in the long evolution of the architecture of simplicity for no other reason than his acknowledged debt to the "poor" architecture of the Mediterranean tradition, the evident influence on his work of masters like Adolf Loos, Mies van der Rohe and, more recently, Tadao Ando, and, lastly, the evidently personal declination of the themes that are pivotal to the work of Silvestrin, Ando and Pawson, namely a sense of space, the rejection of all that is not essential and the value of natural light.

In a complex circumlocution, Campo Baeza's work has been introduced as follows: "The poetics of Campo Baeza... is fuelled by a dense and free dialogue with history, from which it derives not only formal models but also composition strategies and questions to which it has identified an answer by reversing Mies van der Rohe's 'precept' "less is more" with "màs con menos". Since this is his goal... the critics have clearly made very superficial attempts to reduce the outcome of Campo Baeza's research to minimalist stylistics, with which the tectonic rigour and luminous poetics of his works have very little in common.

Having simplified the combination of geometric forms, Campo Baeza's buildings carry the rejection of decoration to extreme consequences, to the point of extenuating it in a painfully hermetic manner.

Avoiding the superfluous... is the raging force of Campo Baeza's works, an anger that is only apparently calmed in the dazzling candour to which his architecture strives or aspires". [112] Leaving aside any uncertainties or contradictions regarding direction, this reasoning presupposes the certified existence of a minimalist movement that has been unequivocally and definitively characterised.

To remove Campo Baeza's work from a wider, albeit clearly differentiated architectural context in which the request for formal simplicity expresses a shared rejection of the convulsed contemporary world, would on the contrary mean reducing his original contribution to an isolated, unattached experience. Something that it really is not.

His work *More with less* exemplifies and clarifies his membership of the broader context.

"I propose an Essential Architecture of Idea, Light and Space.
Idea.
An Architecture that is born of an Idea.
Without an Idea, Architecture would be pointless, only empty form.
An Idea which is capable of serving (function), responding to a place (context), resolving itself geometrically (composition), materialising itself physically (construction).
Light.
An Architecture is brought into existence by Light.
Without Light Architecture is nothing.
Light is an essential material in the construction of Architecture.
Light is that which creates a relation, a tension between man and Architectural space.
Space.
An Architecture is translated into an Essential Space.
Space is shaped by Form through the minimal, indispensable number of ele-ments capable of translating the Idea with precision.
A Space is capable of Touching people.
More with Less".

The introduction to the anthological collection of his most important writings, La idea construida. *La arquitectura a la luz de las palabras* (Madrid 1996), is sufficiently explicit. "Architecture is idea expressed through forms", writes Campo Baeza. "It is the built idea. The history of architecture, far from being only a history of forms, is a history of built ideas. Forms are destroyed by time: but ideas remain and are eternal". There are two fundamental 'ideas' in Campo Baeza's design activities, two concepts that emerge in his poetics to provide the foundations for his composition: light and gravity.

"Gravity builds space, light builds time, and gives reason to time. These are the central questions of architecture: control of gravity and dialogue with light. The future of architecture depends on a new possible understanding of these two phenomena. The future and destiny of this challenging occupation for homo faber can only be the attainment of "Beauty", in the architect's wishes, but by definition it is located "outside" space and time and, therefore, aspiration to classicism, tension towards a knowledge solely limited by the epistemological boundaries of the model". [113]

It is no coincidence that the critics have identified Campo Baeza's most original contribution and his most rigorous adhesion to the principles formulated above in a small, restricted series of works, including those of minor importance. Leaving aside his early works like the Garcia del Valle house (1974), the Fominaya house (1974), the Centre for Professional Education in Pamplona (1974), the Centre for Professional Education in Salamanca (1975), Laboral University in Almeria (1976), the project for the gymnasium at the Ciudad Universitaria in Madrid (1982), the school in San Sebastian de los Reyes (1983) and the school complex at Aluche (1984), in which the architect shows an excessive influence of the Modern Movement, from Mies van der Rohe to Alvar Aalto, coupled with contemporary intrusions (T. Ando, A. Natalini), his first real moment of full adhesion to the rediscovery for the need for clarity and constructive simplicity was the Turégano house of 1988.

Even if not forgetful of Adolf Loos' teachings, a particular modern tradition and the results achieved by the architects of London Minimum, Campo Baeza managed to convey this building towards an ideal of timeless, classic beauty that had been pursued for many years and which, although spoilt by the formalisms of the "Five Architects NY", found an earlier, clear antecedent in the kindergarten in Aspe of 1982.

In a successful progression, Campo Baeza subsequently completed the Marcos house (1991), the Spanish Embassy at Algiers (1992), the Gaspar House (1992), the Drago school in Cadiz (1992), the Balear Centre for Innovative Technologies in Majorca (1995) and the De Blas house in Madrid (2000).

Works, all centripetal towards the courtyard or internal spaces with double-height volumes, in which natural light, whose diagonal rays are exalted, plays a decisive role. The glaring Mediterranean light dematerialises the masonry walls, reduced to volatile white surfaces, and invades the geometric interiors and external areas surrounded by octagonal walls, magnifying a sophisticated effect of metaphysical stillness.

A metaphysical stillness averse to excessive ontological concerns, mitigated by the use of essentially poor materials and condescending to the rhythms of a life in which nature is particularly benign. An idea, in fact.

REORGANISATION OF PIAZZA DEL DUOMO, ALMERIA, 1978–2000.

"This is the winning project in a national open competition organized in 1978. The jury noted as its highest virtues its global vision of the problem and its resolution with the maximum economy of means.

The competition addresses the reorganisation of the Cathedral Square in Almeria. A simple architecture 'without architecture' is proposed. The ground is paved with white Micael marble, the same as the sidewalk paving in the rest of the city. Twenty-four palm trees, taller than the cathedral itself, are located, which, like the columns of an airship, order the space presided over by the renaissance façade by Juan de Orea, as if it were an altarpiece.

The intention is to take 'more with less' to its most radical extreme". (A. Campo Baeza)

Town Hall, Fene, 1980.
"In an area of dispersed buildings lacking a consolidated urban fabric, the creation of two squares, formed by the architectural pieces containing the required functions of the city hall, is proposed. The rectangular site is delineated by three roads and a forest on one of the long sides. The main building, with its easily recognizable symbolic elements, 'the clock tower' and 'the mayor's balcony,' is located at the center, between the two squares. One of these has a more restful character and the other a more cultural.

The central building is quite transparent, very open to the north, and somewhat closed to the south. The whole is resolved by a formally contained and simple, white, architecture, which together with stone architecture is the most common in this area of the country". (A. Campo Baeza)

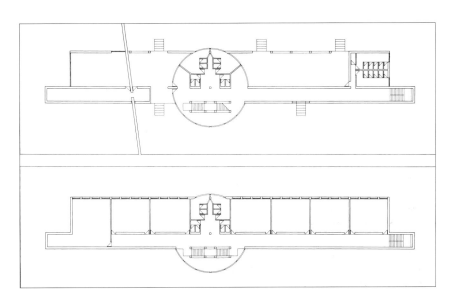

SCHOOL IN SAN FERMIN, MADRID, 1985.
"In response to a precise educational program and strict building codes, the building is an eloquent lineal piece. It appears as a thick rampart wall closed to the north, where the corridor extends, and open to the south, to the sun, where the classrooms lie.

As the junction of both horizontal and vertical circulation, the hall needs to expand and thus ruptures the wall appearing as a cylindrical volume. This triple height interior, which the various levels overlook, is presided over by a transparent stair that allows for an adequate perusal of the space. The usage of glassblock for the enclosure wall converts the hall into a space filled with diffuse northern light which is tensed by well-aimed spots of direct southern light that pierce the transparent skylights". (A. Campo Baeza)

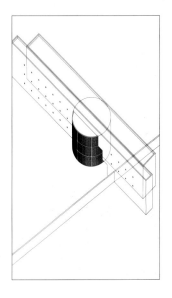

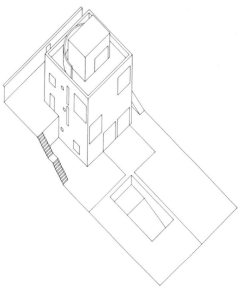

Turegano House, Madrid, 1988.

"The topography, midway down a hillside, the rigorous compliance with building codes, and the maximum economy of means were compositionally resolved in a white cubic 'hut' that measures 10 x 10 x 10 meters.

The white cube is divided in two: the northern half, with the service areas, and the southern half, with the served spaces. The first includes a central strip with bathrooms, water-closets, and stairs. The bedrooms and the kitchen face directly north. The living room and dining room, located in the served half, are of double height, with the study in the highest point. The study peers over the dining room, which in turn looks upon the living room, thus producing a diagonal space of triple height. The cubic nature of this white hut is accentuated by the window glazings flush with the facade, and by the colour white with which all is resolved.

Light, the central theme of this house, is gathered, captured, by windows and slots as it makes its journey from east to south-west, becoming, in its movement, the spatial protagonist of this project. Simply, it is a diagonal space pierced by a diagonal light". (A. Campo Baeza)

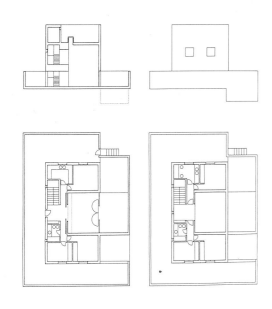

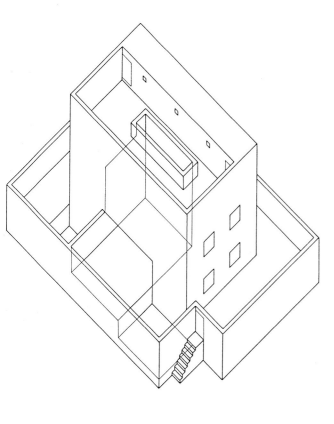

MARCOS HOUSE, MADRID, 1991.

"A single-family house in a conventional suburb on the outskirts of Valdemoro, Madrid is sited on a lot measuring 15 x 21 meters, on a corner with two street facades.

The site is enclosed with walls, like a box open to sky. In the center, complying with set-back requirements, is placed a white prism with a rectangular base of 8 x 14 meters.

This box is organized by a central double height space that is diagonally pierced by the convergence of Light; a vertical light entering through a skylight in the ceiling stretching from side to side, and a low horizontal light which enters through a large window also extending from side to side.

Through Light and Proportion, a small and simple closed house, is converted into a grand and open house, where, with almost nothing, everything is possible. 'Une boîte à miracles', a miracle box". (A. Campo Baeza)

GASPAR HOUSE, ZAHORA, CADIZ, 1992.

"The client's main wish was for complete independence. It was decided, therefore, to create an enclosed area, a 'hortus conclusus'. One proceeds from an 18 x 18m square defined by four 3.5m-high patio walls, which is divided in three equal parts. Only the central part is roofed over. Divided transversally in three parts, with the proportions A/2A/A, by two low walls, the service elements are included in the side areas. The roof of the central space is made higher, 4.5m. At the points of intersection between the low walls and the high walls are four 2 x 2m apertures, which are glazed. Through these four apertures the horizontal plane of the stone floor spreads out, thus providing an effective exterior-interior continuity.

The white color of all the wall faces contributes to the clarity and continuity of this architecture. The symmetry of the composition remains evident, due to the placement, also symmetrical, of four lemon trees, which produce mirror effects.

The LIGHT in this house is horizontal and continuous, reflected on the walls of the east-west oriented patios. In short, this is a continuous HORIZONTAL space, tensed by a HORIZONTAL light". (A. Campo Baeza)

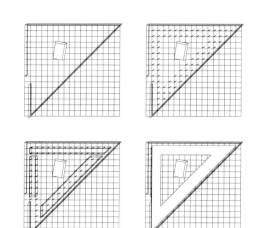

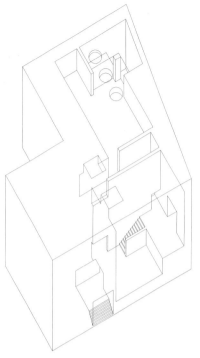

Drago School, Cadiz, 1992.

"This building, with its great white facade overlooking the sea, is conceived as a continuation of the long and extensive white walls of the old 'maritime' cemetery of Cadiz.

The irregular trapezoidal site is regularized through the efficient mechanism of a square courtyard around which the circulation winds. Its square form is accentuated by four palms arranged on its stone paving.

The more public spaces are located in the part of the building which looks to the sea, and are more intensely controlled. A deep, double order opening, expresses to the city the public nature of the building, and groups together the library and cafeteria spaces. The shadowed depth is tensed by the solid sunlight captured by the high circular skylight.

The space which hierarchically presides over the building is the main triple height hall where all of the circulation patterns converge. Its verticality is tensed by diagonal light from the high skylights, and made continuous by the eye-opening to the sea, supported by an intermediate plane which makes that view possible. A vertical space tensed by a diagonal light". (A. Campo Baeza)

Centre for Innovative Technologies, Inca, Majorca, 1995.

"The program entails the construction of high tech office space on a triangular site within an industrial park, for which a garden is created. Following the triangular outline of the site, a high wall of 'mares' stone is raised to form an enclosed area. The site is then completely excavated at the basement level and the horizontal plane re-established above by a floor slab finished in travertine marble, the same as the interior finish of the walls. A box of travertine open to the sky is thus formed, upon which an orthogonal grid 6 x 6 meters is drawn.

Separated from the walls, a band parallel to the sides of the triangle is formed by cylindrical white metallic columns on top of which is placed a flat roof that cantilevers 2 meters on either side. This space is enclosed with frameless glazing, creating a space that is continuous with the horizontal travertine ground plane. The remaining points marked by the grid are planted with fragrant vegetation: orange trees. On the walls climbing plants with aromatic blossoms are trained: jasmine, wisteria, and grapevine. A garden is thus created, a 'secret garden' in whose interior the work spaces are placed. The composition is tensed by the placement of the conference room, conveniently shifted, at the center: a space with tiers of seating excavated into the stone floor and covered by a glazed box. All of the service conduits flow through the basement, 'piercing' through the ground to the work spaces when necessary. Once more an architecture with a stereotomic stone base is created, an inverted podium supporting the lighter tectonic elements; the whole tuned with the utmost precision and the maximum economy of means". (A. Campo Baeza)

De Blas House, Madrid, 2000.
"Placed on the crest of a north-facing hill with views to the mountains near Madrid, the house, more than anything, is a response to this location to settle a platform.

A concrete box was built, a platform upon which to sit. A transparent glass box, roofed by a delicate and light steel structure, painted in white, is placed upon this podium. One with the earth, the poured-in-place concrete box like a cave houses the program of a traditional house with a clear diagram of served spaces to the front and service spaces to the rear. The glass box is placed upon the platform, like a hut, a belvedere to which one rises from within the house.

In the upper part of the house, I worked on the horizontal light crossing the horizontal space. Basic subjects here, are the transparency and continuous space.

The landscape of the mountains to the north of the house is illuminated by the south light. The spectator, under cover in the shade, contemplates the view, lighted, UNDERLINED in such a way that it comes towards him. In the lower part of the house, in the cave, I worked with the light framed by the interior shadow.

The landscape of the mountains, illuminated outside is FRAMED in such a way that it escapes from the spectator. That's how light illuminating the landscape, underlined or framed by the shade, shows up as an efficient architectural mechanism.

Below, the cave is a refuge. Above the hut, an urn, is a space from which to contemplate nature. The entire project is conformed by the precision of its dimensions. The concrete box is 9 by 27 meters. The metallic structure is 6 x 15 meters. The glass box is 4.5 x 9 meters by 2.26 meters high.

This house attempts to be a literal translation of a tectonic box set upon a stereotomic question: a tectonic piece set upon a stereotomic box. A distillation of what is essential in architecture. Once again, 'more with less'". (A. Campo Baeza)

HEAD OFFICE OF THE CAJA GENERAL DE AHORROS, GRANADA, 1992–2001.

"The central offices of the Caja General de Ahorros de Granada, the city's most important bank, are to stand in the ill-defined outskirts of Granada.

A huge, semi-cubic volume is proposed which may serve as a reference for tensing this part of the city. In order to accommodate the slope of the land and to resolve the unevenness of the ground, which looks over the two roads skirting it, a large base is created on which the semi-cubic mass is seated. Parking areas and services are resolved in the podium. The protruding box, a stereotomic box, is constructed with a 3 x 3 x 3m reinforced-concrete grid that serves as a mechanism for garnering the light, a central theme of this architecture. The two south facades function as a brise-soleil and illuminate, by nuancing that potent light, the open office areas. The two north facades, serving the individual offices, receive the homogeneous, continuous light specific to that orientation and are closed off from the outside with a revêtement of travertine marble and glass.

The roofed central atrium, a true 'impluvium of light', garners the solid south light through the skylights and, reflecting this in the alabaster facings, complements the illumination of the open-plan offices. Functionally speaking, the building is characterised by enormous compactness, flexibility and simplicity.

To sum up, this is a self-contained stereotomic box of concrete and glass that traps the light from the south in its interior, thereby serving a further tectonic box immersed in an effective 'impluvium of light'. A diagonal space traversed by diagonal light". (A. Campo Baeza)

MICHAEL GABELLINI

Gabellini is recognized for his signature design utilizing a simplicity of means in relation to form and function. By rendering space, light and materials as palpable entities, Gabellini distills the craft of design into an intuitive, yet technical art form.

The years at the Rhode Island School of Design as well as the Architectural Association in London, where he studied architecture and design, but foremost, painting and sculpture, in addition to the many Italian visits, were decisive.

In Rome he first came in contact with the Panza collection in 1978, adding Arte Povera to his knowledge of the American minimalist artists of the 60's. While in Italy his fascination with ancient cultures and in particular archaeology was enhanced. Typologies and methods of construction used by the Romans and Etruscans became the object of academic and cultural interest.

In the Etruscan necropolises, where the dead are surrounded by objects of daily life and spaces that recreate a habitat that is similar to that of life on earth, Gabellini found the key for his future work: to introduce light and motion into the urban spaces of the metropolis where most human activities are concentrated.

His early formation as a sculptor and his attraction to the work of the California Light Artists such as Dan Flavin, James Turrell, Larry Bell and Robert Irwin and the American Minimalist artists of the 60's influenced Gabellini toward a conception of the architectural discipline as conceptual space and the awareness that the results obtained by minimalism in art cannot be transposed directly to pure form.

In addition to his preference for the work of architects such as R. Neutra, L. Kahn and Mies van der Rohe, whom he admired and considered unsurpassed masters of simplicity and formal reduction, he has greatly reflected on ancient cultures and the secular building tradition of the architecture of simplicity.

At the end of the 80's Gabellini adhered with considerable awareness to the emerging tendency of architectural minimalism, refuting the more reductive version that sees in this phenomenon a pure expression of style and emphasizing instead the great complexity and profound nature of this choice that is foremost a way of life.

"Many people think that minimalist art or architecture is something cold, abstract and sterile. Instead minimalism is not only art or architecture, actually it is an idea that does not dilute existence. It is analogous to the editing of film, where there is an inherent concentration of form and experience. More than a subtraction, minimalism is an inherent concentration of experience and pleasure." [114]

In reference to Gabellini's work one should really speak of maximalism: the difficulty of representing reduction in architecture leading to a synthesis of formal simplicity and experience.

The theatrical work of Robert Wilson is acknowledged as fundamental. Notwithstanding differences of means and intents, the influence of the "Master of Light" can undoubtedly be seen in Gabellini's interiors. Conceiving interior space as a theatrical black box where artificial light plays a key role, Gabellini introduces narrative and the illusion of reality and natural light (obtained almost exclusively with artificial means and therefore in an abstract and conceptual way) into contemporary, dimensionless and timeless spaces. Gabellini attempts to reintroduce in his spaces a refined perception, whose main elements are light, air and sound. Using careful control of these basic elements Gabellini achieves results that substantiate a more general minimalist tendency to create calm and tranquil spaces." Just like in the theater, if you turn on a single light you feel a sense of time, space and an emotional state. In architecture it is very important to achieve an elemental space that is able to enhance the elements of daily life."

In 1991 Gabellini founded Gabellini Associates that specializes in showrooms, art galleries, and exhibition design. Gabellini's approach to design, whether for private residences, civic spaces, art galleries or fashion boutiques, is defined by a specific set of criteria: the unique needs of each individual client and the specific context of the project, the development of a seamless and sophisticated background for the programmatic requirements, and the creation of an aesthetically pure environment.

Working with space and light as sculptural materials, Gabellini constructs architectural settings that are at once elemental in form and dramatic in their purity of means. An essential reductivism, attention to detail and sensitivity to the intrinsic properties of building material and location identify the studio's signature vocabulary. This 'minimalist' sensibility evolves not from a predetermined architectural style but, rather, from the intent to design pure functional spaces that operate as backdrops to what is contained within them. Formal simplicity requires intellectual rigor and aesthetic restraint. The end result lies in the creation of environments that are opulent in the clarity of their spatial resolution.

For Michael Gabellini, the operative metaphor is of the mis-en-scène. Each building, urban setting or interior space is designed as a platform for the action within. As in theater, the backdrops must be flexible and understated enough to foreground the dramatic event. Yet, they must also articulate a specific atmosphere or temporal moment while providing a visually coherent setting. To this end, Gabellini often utilizes mutable components and custom designed, state-of-the-art lighting systems that focus and highlight their buildings' programmatic elements. Although the technologies that Gabellini makes use of are of the most sophisticated type and are often custom-designed, they are invisible within the development of the architecture. To extend the theatrical metaphor, Gabellini creates the illusion of seamless space.

The studio's most important private commissions include worldwide concepts for fashion designers Jil Sander, Giorgio Armani, Salvatore Ferragamo, Gianfranco Ferri and Nicole Farhi. In addition, Gabellini has been involved with exhibition and gallery design for institutions which include the Solomon R. Guggenheim Museum, the Cooper-Hewitt National Design Museum, Marion Goodman Gallery, Grant Selwyn Fine Art and the Casey Kaplan Gallery in New York. The sophisticated luxury of the interior for the Paris Jil Sander boutique on Avenue Montaigne exemplifies the basic paradox of minimal architecture: that what may appear formally simple is actually tremendously complex, requiring intense attention to detail and the highest quality finishes and artisan labor to create an environment of subtle but penetrating beauty. The same can be said about the enigmatic interior of Grant Selwyn Fine Art Gallery in New York, where for one installation, work by Donald Judd and Dan Flavin conspire to illuminate the complimentary nature between art and architecture. In the studio's residential projects such as 785 Park Avenue, a refined understated environment provides a tranquil backdrop for the serene enjoyment of daily living.

While Gabellini's projects largely involved the development of interior architectural environments from the 1980's through the first half of the 1990's, the studio's recent commissions include the award-winning urban design competition for the Piazza Isolo in Verona, three private residences under development in America and an upcoming 12-story luxury hotel in San Francisco.

Through the development of exclusive retail, exhibition and residential projects over the last 12 years, Gabellini has used architectural design as a platform to express a unique sense of volumetric harmony through the interaction of light, space and materials. In order to create a concept of 'emotional space', defined by a transcendent tactile and physical presence, Gabellini is able to make each environment a seamless frame through which experience is heightened, leading to an overall suspension of time and place.

DENTE RESIDENCE, NEW YORK, NY 1985.
IN COLLABORATION WITH JAY SMITH
"This 200 square meter penthouse residence with panoramic views of lower Manhattan represents one of Gabellini's first significant minimalist projects. An environment of functional simplicity is conceived spatially as two white volumes connected by a white marble stair. These hovering volumes are defined by a reductive palette of white French plaster walls and ceilings and honed white Sivec marble floors slabs, which emphasize the luminosity of the volumes and the transcendent malleability from day to evening. In this way, light is seen as the temporal and transforming element of the spare contemplative space.
Openly connecting the living room to the bedroom on the lower level, the stair, conceived as a floating ribbon, is composed of a sequence of cascading marble platforms supported on a single steel riser winding gracefully and rhythmically from one space to another. Throughout the apartment, the calm tranquility is reflected in all design elements from the bath to the display of art". (Gabellini Associates)

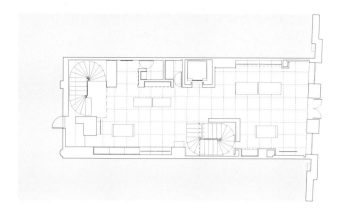

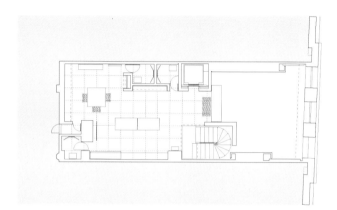

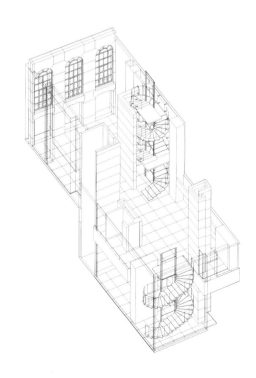

JIL SANDER FLAGSHIP BOUTIQUE, PARIS, 1993.
"This 1,000 square-meter boutique and showroom on four levels on Avenue Montaigne in Paris was the first of a continuing collaboration between Gabellini and Jil Sander, which defined the elemental quality of the Jil Sander worldwide retail concept.
Set in what once was a quintessential Beaux Arts Hotel Particulier of the 1890's, and after its many conversions, Gabellini's restorative act imposed harmonic order to the interior that established a dialogue between old and new by revealing its classical proportions and grand spatial quality. The physical space is articulated by three monolithic marble columns, which act as sectional elements of movement. The refined environment has a specially designed lighting system that renders volumetric forms and various materials as separate but interrelated entities. With these defining elements, the monumental atrium wall, the understated use of elegant materials and lighting, and the interplay between gravity and weightlessness is achieved". (Gabellini Associates)

JIL SANDER OFFICES AND SHOWROOM, HAMBURG, 1996.
"Situated in a private park on the banks of the Alster Lake in Hamburg, the 1,800 square-meter mid-nineteenth century villa required extensive restoration to host the worldwide Jil Sander show-room, design studios and executive offices. While the quality of the villa and the details suggested a historic restoration of the Belle Etage, the program of the showroom and offices demanded radical restructuring.

Gabellini's approach was to maintain the balance between old and new. On the main levels a meticulous restoration of the plaster reliefs and woodwork was executed with a bold but unobtrusive hand, whereas the lower level was excavated to create new spaces for meeting rooms, dining areas, a kitchen and buffet and an exterior dining terrace. In contrast to the upper floors, this space is designed in the signature pure vocabulary of the Jil Sander design concept, where space, light and materials interact to create a space of elegance and animated tranquility. The weaving together of old and new is furthered by the use of Spanish Arria limestone floors and furnishings and fixtures throughout the space". (Gabellini Associates)

JIL SANDER BOUTIQUE, SAN FRANCISCO, 1996.
"Within a landmark building in downtown San Francisco, Gabellini designed two highly contrasting, yet complementary retail spaces for the same client: Ultimo of Chicago. The 450 square-
meter Jil Sander Flagship Boutique shares the Jil Sander signature spatial vocabulary defined by
pure, linear geometries, translucent, light-filled planes and floating surfaces. The boutique features a double-height atrium space which allowed for the creation of a sweeping interior facade
penetrated by northern light. The spatial concept created an environment of open, sun lit planes
suspended by a shaded ceiling canopy allowing the collection to float freely within the space".
(Gabellini Associates)

ULTIMO BOUTIQUE, SAN FRANCISCO, 1996.

"The 350 square-meter Ultimo Boutique, adjacent to Jil Sander, is conceived as a red chinoiserie box within which a vaulted ivory ceiling plane floats to conceal ambient lighting which spills onto the walls and perimeter vitrines as luminescent veils of projected light. A ramp and bluestone display platform lead to a stair placed between a silicon bronze wall and a two-story wall of translucent Rosa Portugalo marble rising through a double height atrium.

The luxurious material palette extends to custom display fixtures designed by Gabellini. Silk scrolls, water white mirror panels and walnut trapeze bars are suspended from the ceiling by black tensile fabric cord. The walnut furniture was designed in collaboration with George Nakashima Woodworkers to create a dramatic backdrop to the different collections on display". (Gabellini Associates)

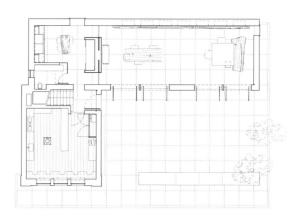

Coleen B. Rosenblat Jewelry Showroom, Hamburg, 1998.

"This 450 square-meter project, comprising a jewelry showroom, design studio and a small apartment is situated in a former carriage house in the historic Poseldorf section of Hamburg. The showroom presented the unique possibilities and challenges of displaying jewelry: highlighting precious gems though the development of atmospheric light and the need for security while maintaining a sense of openness and accessibility. The display cases were conceived as miniature mis-en-scenés carved out of a masonry wall in the showroom and united by a 12 meter long American walnut shelf. Recessed fiberoptic lighting and a sliding groove allow the line of glass to float freely in front of the display wall creating the sensation of a suspended optical plane.

In contrast to the precious stones and metals on display, the palette chosen by Gabellini is expressed by four materials: traditional imperial plaster, honed Spanish limestone, translucent optical glass and wenge heartwood. Each material was chosen for its chromatic uniformity and its character of light against which the gemstones radiate". (Gabellini Associates)

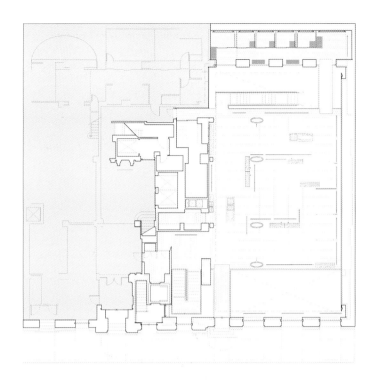

NICOLE FARHI BOUTIQUE, NEW YORK, 1999.
"Located in midtown in Manhattan, the 2,000 square-meter boutique, showroom and restaurant occupy three levels of a 1901 landmark building.

Entry to the boutique begins with a passage across a floating bridge of water-white glass and American walnut wood. The bridge spans the front atrium, revealing the interior architectural plaster façade. Between this and another double-height atrium at the rear, the floor of the women's boutique is suspended within the space. The women's collection is punctuated by four large elliptical plaster columns which continue to the floor below. Access to the lower level boutique and restaurant is made possible by a front and rear floating wooden stair.

On the lower level, a 400 square-meter restaurant is placed between the two double-height atrium spaces. Its main elements are a 10-meter-long luminescent bar table carved from Estremoz, a translucent Portuguese marble, and an illuminated water-white glass cube housing the open kitchen floating on a raised bluestone plinth". (Gabellini Associates)

GRANT SELWYN FINE ART GALLERY, NEW YORK, 1999.
"Located in midtown Manhattan, this 250 square-meter gallery exhibits contemporary painting, sculpture, works on paper, individual artist installations and group shows. The flexible yet intimate program demanded a complete reconfiguration of the space's interior to maximize the exhibition space while providing office, library, archive and storage space.
A 360° pivoting wall that floats between floor and ceiling on a single ball-bearing mechanism was devised to offer flexibility in displaying differing artistic media with varying scales and technical requirements as well as defining the space as one or two areas. Gabellini's design concept treats
the space as a frame to the art on display: a composition of space, form and material with refined attention to detail.
The lighting system has been carefully designed to be flexible and sensitive to the dual need of lighting the space itself and the artwork within. A
continuous ambient perimeter light cove wraps the entire gallery creating a luminescent veil of light in which the ceiling appears to float in the 4-
meter space, whereas recessed fixtures directly light the artwork on display". (Gabellini Associates)

NOTES

1. F. Quadri, F. Bertoni, R. Stearns, *Robert Wilson*, Octavo, Firenze 1997
2. K. Robert Schwarz, *Minimalists*, Phaidon, London 1966
3. F. Carmagnola, V. Pasca, *Minimalismo*, Lupetti, Milano 1996
4. F. Carmagnola, V. Pasca, op.cit., p.169
5. J. Graham, *System and Dialectics of Art*, Baltimore 1971, p.115
6. F Carmagnola, V. Pasca, op.cit., p. 169
7. B. Lattati, Introduzione, in R.Carver, *Cattedrale*, Mondadori, Milano 1984, p.VI
8. B. Lattati, op.cit., p. VII
9. F. Pivano, Il Minimalismo di Raymond Carver, in R. Carver, *Di cosa parliamo quando parliamo d'amore*, Garzanti, Milano 1987, p.145
10. R. Carver, *Where I'm Calling from*. The Selected Stories, London 1993, p.XIV
11. T. Mann, *Last Essays, Chekhov*, London 1959, p.203
12. F. Carmagnola, V. Pasca, op.cit., p. 102
13. F. Carmagnola, V. Pasca, op.cit., p.102
14. A. Loos, *Parole nel vuoto*, Adelphi, Milano 1972, p.186
15. F. Neumeyer, *The Artless Word. Mies van der Rohe on the Building Art*, London 1991
16. R. Guardini, *Letters from Lake Como*, Edinburgh 1994
17. R. Guardini, op.cit., pp.5–6
18. R. Guardini. op.cit., p.78
19. R. Guardini, op.cit., p.78

20. F. Neumeyer, op.cit., p. 200
21. R. Guardini, op.cit., p.79
22. R. Guardini, op.cit., p.92
23. R. Guardini, op.cit., p.88
24. F. Neumeyer, op.cit., p. 208
25. U. Galimberti, *Nessun Dio ci può salvare*, in 'Micromega' n.2/2000, p.187
26. F. Bertoni, *Claudio Silvestrin*, Octavo, Firenze 1999, p.164
27. F. Bertoni, op.cit., p.165
28. F. Carmagnola, V. Pasca, op.cit., p.174
29 F. Carmagnola, V. Pasca, op.cit., p.167
30 A. Vettese, 'Semplicità minimale nell'arte: fiume carsico o movimento specifico?', in F. Carmagnola, V. Pasca, op.cit., p.169
31. F. Carmagnola, V. Pasca, op.cit., p.29
32. F. Carmagnola, V. Pasca, op.cit., p.178
33. F. Carmagnola, V. Pasca, op.cit., p.178
34. F. Carmagnola, V. Pasca, op.cit., p.178
35. F. Neumeyer, op.cit., pp.204
36. F. Neumeyer, op.cit., p.203
37. F. Neumeyer, op.cit., p.204
38. F. Neumeyer, op.cit., p.204
39. E. Battisti, 'L'Angelico e l'impegno', in AA.VV., *Angelico a San Marco*, Curcio, Roma 1965
40. J. Pawson, *minimum*, Phaidon, London 1996
41. F. Quadri, F. Bertoni, R. Stearns, op.cit., p.232

42. F. Bertoni, *Claudio Silvestrin*, op.cit., pp.203–225
43. T. N. Kinder, *I Cistercensi*, Jaca Book, Milano 1997
   R. Toman (ed.), *L'arte del romanico*, Konemann, Cologne 1996 J.-F. Leroux-Dhuis, *Cistercian Abbeys*, Konemann, Cologne 1998
44. G. Duby, *San Bernardo e l'arte cistercense*, Einaudi, Torino 1982
45. G. Duby, op.cit., p.76
46. G. Duby, op.cit., p.76
47. G. Duby, op.cit., p.92
48. G. Duby, op.cit., p.113
49. G. Duby, op.cit., p.128
50. G. Duby, op.cit., p.138
51. G. Duby, op.cit., p.145
52. E. Panofsky, *Perspective as symbolic form*, New York 1991, p.52
53. G. Duby, op.cit., p.184
54. AA.VV., *Giuseppe Pistocchi, architetto giacobino*, Faenza 1974
55. F. Dal Co, *Tadao Ando, Complete Works*, London 1995
56. P. Ranzo, 'L'era del *ma*', in F. Carmagnola, op.cit., p.147
57. F. Bertoni, *Claudio Silvestrin*, op.cit., p.179
58. L. Benevolo, *History of Modern Architecture*, vol.I, London 1971, p.144
59. G. C. Argan, *L'arte moderna 1770/1970*, Sansoni, Firenze 1970, p.87
60. G. C. Argan, op.cit., p.115

61. G. C. Argan, op.cit., p.122
62. J. Rykwert, *The Necessity of Artefice, Adolf Loos*, Academy Editions, London 1982, p.73
63. P. Ranzo, op.cit., p.149
64. B. Gravagnuolo, *Il mito mediterraneo nell'architettura contemporanea*, Electa, Napoli 1994, p.7
65. B. Gravagnuolo, op.cit., p.14
66. E. Godoli-G. Fanelli, *La Vienna di Hoffmann architetto della qualità*, Laterza, Bari 1981, p.10
67. J. Hoffmann. *The Architectural Works*, ed. E.F. Sekler, Princeton 1985, p.479
68. B. Gravagnuolo, op.cit., p.17
    M. McDonough, *Malaparte. a house like me*, Clarkson Potter/Publishers, New York 1999
69. F. Braudel, *La Mediterranée. L'espace et l'histoire*, Paris 1977, p.7
70. P. Ranzo, op.cit., p.152
71. W. Kandinsky, *Tutti gli scritti*, Feltrinelli, Milano 1973
72. W. Worringer, *Abstraction and empathy*, London 1953, p.15; pp.19–20
73. K. Malevic, *Suprematismo*, Laterza, Bari 1969
74. F. Bertoni, op.cit., p.186
75. V. Cerami, *C'era una volta il rumore del silenzio*, in 'La Repubblica' del 24.IX.1998
76. M. Toy, *practically minimal*. Thames and Hudson, London 2000
A. Cuito, *Interni minimalisti*, Logos, Modena 2000

A. Cuito, *Loft minimalisti*, Logos, Modena 2001
77. F. Bertoni, op.cit.
78. A. Campo Baeza, *La idea construida*, Colegio Oficial de Arquitectos, Madrid 1996
79. J. Pawson, *minimum*, op.cit.
80. F. Dal Co, op.cit.
81. F. Bertoni, op.cit., p.165
82. F. Dal Co, op.ct., p.444
83. F. Dal Co, op.cit., p.448
84. J. Pawson, op.cit., p.7
85. F. Carmagnola-V. Pasca, op.cit., p.102
86. Architectural Design, *Aspects of minimal architecture*, London 1994
87. *Peter Zumthor Works. Buildings and Projects 1979–1997*, Birkhäuser, Basel 1999
88. M. Vignelli, in F.Bertoni, op.cit., p.226
89. P. Altenberg, *Favole della vita*, Adelphi, Milano 1981, p.265
90. Luis Barragan, *The Quiet Revolution*, edited by Federica Zanco, Skyra, Milano, 2001
91. Barragan, *The Complete Works*, London 1996, pp.204–07
92. T. Mann, *Last Essays, Chekhov*, London 1959, p.203
93. F. Carmagnola, V. Pasca, op.cit.
94. Ruedi Baur, *Projets, exhibition catalogue*, Lyon Villeurbanne 1986
95. F. Carmagnola, V. Pasca, op.cit.

96. Francesco Dal Co, *Tadao Ando, Complete Works*, 1995, p.504
97. Francesco Dal Co, op. cit., p.445
98. Francesco Dal Co, op. cit., p.448
99. Francesco Dal Co, op. cit., p.7–8
100. Francesco Dal Co, op. cit., p.444
101. Francesco Dal Co, op. cit., p.444
102. F. Bertoni, Cop. cit., p.164
103. Bruce Chatwin, 'Wabi', in John Pawson, *GG*, Barcelona 1998
104. Deyan Sudjic, Introduction, in John Pawson, op. cit.
105. Deyan Sudjic, Introduction, in John Pawson, op. cit.
106. W. Worringer, op. cit., p.16
107. W. Worringer, op. cit., p.19
108. Michael Speaks, *Rigorously Sensual Minimalism, Critic vol.3*, Osaka 1995
109. W. Worringer, op. cit., p.16
110. John Pawson, *minimum*, Phaidon, London 1996
111. *Peter Zumthor Works. Buildings and Projects 1979–1997*, Birkhäuser, Basel 1999
112. *Alberto Campo Baeza*, Electa, Milano 1999
113. *Alberto Campo Baeza*, op. cit., p. 12
114. Comments made to author by Gabellini Associates

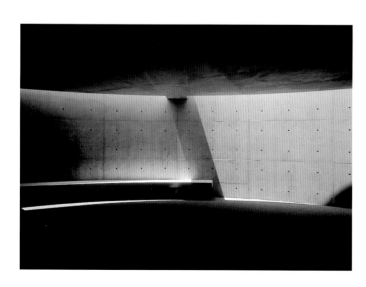

LUIS BARRAGÁN

Born in Guadalajara, Mexico, in 1902.
He travelled to Europe and the United States in 1925 and 1931. After making his professional debut in 1927, influenced by traditional Mexican architecture, he drew closer to the experience of the Modern Movement.
After the Second World War, he embarked on a personal research project that was internationally acclaimed at a personal exhibition organised by Emilio Ambasz at the Museum of Modern Art in New York in 1976.
He was awarded the American Prize for Architecture in 1987.
He died in Mexico City in 1988.
Bibl.: F. Zanco (ed.), *Luis Barragan. The quiet revolution*, Skira and Barragan Foundation, 2001 (with full bibliography)

AG FRONZONI

Born in Pistoia, Italy in 1923.
He studied at Brescia from 1945 to 1955 and then in Milan from 1956. Owing to his pre-eminently graphic interests, he became editor of Casabella from 1965 to 1967, but did not neglect his teaching activities at the Umanitaria in Milan from 1967 to 1969, at the Istituto Statale d'Arte in Monza from 1968, at the Istituto Superiore per le Industrie Artistiche in Urbino from 1975 to 1977, at the Istituto di Comunicazione Visiva in Milan from 1978 to 1979, as well as holding private courses in his own workshop.
In addition to being a graphic artist and designer, AG Fronzoni is also an interior designer.
Bibl.: R. Baur, *AG Fronzoni*, Galleria Projets, Lyon, 1986

TADAO ANDO

Born in Osaka, Japan, in 1941.
A self-taught architect, he travelled extensively in Europe, Africa and the United States. In 1969 he started to work professionally and in 1972 he made the first of a long series of single family residences. Azuma House (1976) drew him to the attention of international criticism. From 1979 onwards, a number of exhibitions held in major museums worldwide, like the Museum of Modern Art in New York and the Centre Pompidou in Paris, have focused on his work. In 1995 Ando was awarded the Pritzker Prize and in 1997 the Royal Gold Medal by the RIBA.
Bibl.: F. Dal Co, *Tadao Ando*, Electa, Milano, 1998 (contains list of his works, bibliography, writings and anthology of criticism).

CLAUDIO SILVESTRIN

Born in 1954 Claudio Silvestrin studied in Milan under AG Fronzoni and continued his studies at the Architectural Association in London, the city where he now lives and works. He worked in collaboration with John Pawson from 1986 to 1988.
The Neuendorf villa in Majorca received international acclaim. Calvin Klein and, above all, Giorgio Armani then commissioned him to design their most prestigious show-rooms.
Bibl.: F. Bertoni, *Claudio Silvestrin*, Octavo, Firenze, 1998

JOHN PAWSON

Born in Halifax, England in 1949. After spending some time working in the family textile business and three years teaching in Japan, he started to study at the Architectural Association of London in his thirties. He collaborated with Claudio Silvestrin from 1986 to 1988. He achieved international recognition through his works for Calvin Klein and for clients in London Minimum. His book *minimum* was published in 1996.
Bibl.: AA.VV., *John Pawson*, Gustavo Gili, Barcelona, 1992, 1998, 1999
D.Sudijc, *John Pawson, Works*, Phaidon, London, 2000

PETER ZUMTHOR

Born in Basel, Switzerland in 1943. Having initially trained as a cabinet-maker, he studied at the Kunstgewerbeschule in Basel and at the Pratt Institute of New York. In 1968 he was employed as an architect in the Department for the Conservation of Monuments in the Canton of Graubünden. He started to work on his own in 1979. Having taught in the United States, Austria, Germany, since 1996 he has been professor at the Academy of Architecture at the University of Italian Switzerland in Mendrisio.
Bibl.: P. Zumthor, *Peter Zumthor, Works*, Birkhäuser, Basel-Boston-Berlin, 1999 (with full bibliography)

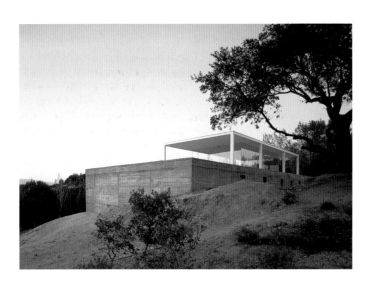

EDUARDO SOUTO DE MOURA

Born in Oporto, Portugal in 1952. While studying at the School of Architecture in Oporto, he worked with Alvaro Siza from 1974 to 1979. After graduating in 1980, he set up his own practice. He has been invited to teach and hold seminars at the most distinguished universities worldwide (Paris, Harvard, Dublin, Zurich, Lausanne) and has exhibited his works in Portugal, France, Italy, United Kingdom and the United States.

Bibl.: AA.VV., *Eduardo Souto Moura*, Blau, Lisbona, 1994

ALBERTO CAMPO BAEZA

Born in Valladolid, Spain in 1946. He graduated in architecture in 1971 from the Escuela Tecnica Superior de Arquitectura in Madrid and embarked on a prolific series of professional activities and an intense schedule of conferences; he also became a visiting professor at several international institutes. In 1997 he became full professor at the Ecole Polytechnique Fédérale of Lausanne and in 1999 at the University of Pennsylvania in Philadelphia.

In 1996 he wrote *La idea construida. La arquitectura a la luz de las parablas*.

Bibl.: *Alberto Campo Baeza*, (with essay by Antonio Pizza), Electa, Milano, 1999 (contains full bibliography).

MICHAEL GABELLINI

Born in Pennsylvania in 1958.

A registered architect and a member of the American Institute of Architects, Michael Gabellini received his Bachelor degree from the Rhode Island School of Design in 1980. He also studied in London and in Rome. Before founding Gabellini Associates in 1991, he worked at Kohn Pederson Fox Architects for six years. During this period, he also collaborated with designer Jay Smith on a number of fashion-related projects.

In 1997, the firm received five American Institute of Architects' Awards. Gabellini Associates was recently honored with I.D. magazine's 1999 award for environmental design.

Bibl.: 'Michael Gabellini', in *Design Culture Now*, March 2000

CONCISE BIBLIOGRAPHY

Minimal, in 'Rassegna' no. 36, Milano 1988
Aspects of Minimal Architecture I, in 'Architectural Design', London 1994
F. Poli, *Minimalismo-Arte Povera-Arte Concettuale*, Laterza, Roma Bari 1995
H. Ypma, *London Minimum*, Thames and Hudson, London 1996
F. Carmagnola-V. Pasca, *Minimalismo*, Lupetti, Milano 1996
J. Pawson, *minimum*, Phaidon, London 1998
Aspects of Minimal Architecture II, in 'Architectural Design', London 1999
M. Toy, *Practically Minimal*, Thames and Hudson, London 2000
A. Zabalbeascoa-J. R. Marcos, *Minimalisms*, Gustavo Gili, Barcelona 2000
J. Meyer, *Minimalism*, Phaidon, London 2000

I would like to thank Myrna Cohen for her help and active collaboration in researching the iconographic material for AG Fronzoni's architectural works, and Mario Nanni, proprietor of Via Bizzuno, Bologna, for providing the photographic material for AG Fronzoni's personal exhibition held in Spazio Calderara, Milan.
I am also grateful to all the architects included in this book for their collaboration and, in particular, to Tadao Ando, Alberto Campo Baeza, Michael Gabellini, Claudio Silvestrin and Eduardo Souto de Moura for having supplied the texts reproduced here.

This book is dedicated to my wife, Jolanda, and my children, Maria and Antonio.

"Que ceci soit la fin du livre – mais non la fin de la recherche"
Saint Bernard